Critical Guides to Spanish Texts

EDITED BY J. E. VAREY AND A. D. DEYERMOND

D1422492

Critical Guides to Spanish Texts

PÍO BAROJA

El mundo es ansí

C. A. Longhurst

Lecturer in Spanish, University of Leeds

Grant & Cutler Ltd *in association with*
Tamesis Books Ltd 1977

© Grant and Cutler Ltd 1977

ISBN 0 7293 0040 4

Printed in England at
The Compton Press Ltd
Tisbury, Wilts.
for
GRANT & CUTLER LTD
11 BUCKINGHAM STREET, LONDON, W.C.2

Contents

Prefatory Note

The interpretation of *El mundo es ansí* that the reader will find
here is to the best of my knowledge an entirely new one. This
Critical Guide has not been conceived primarily as a guide to
existing criticism – criticism of specific novels of Baroja is in any
case scant and *El mundo es ansí* is no exception – but has been
born rather out of my own dissatisfaction with most existing criticism and out of my belief that if we abandon all critical preconcep-
tions about Baroja's art and devote our energies instead to a close
study of the novels we may yet see Baroja in a quite different
light. Far from being a deadpan realist who should have been
writing many decades earlier, Baroja was, I believe, acutely in
tune with the major artistic preoccupations of his time and may
well have been the most 'modern' of his generation of writers.
Baroja was living at a time when the nature and function of the
novel was under review, not just in Spain but in the whole of the
Western world, and *El mundo es ansí* is, as I hope to show, very
much a product of its age. I have therefore thought it necessary,
before embarking on the study of *El mundo es ansí*, to inform or
to remind the reader of some of the basic issues of early twentieth-
century fiction.

The figures in parentheses in italic type refer to the numbered
items in the Bibliographical Note; where appropriate, the italicised
figures are followed by page numbers. Page references on their
own refer to the edition of *El mundo es ansí* prepared by D. L.
Shaw and published by Pergamon Press, Oxford, 1970. Quota-
tions from other works of Baroja are taken from the *Obras com-
pletas* (8 vols, 1947–51) and are indicated by the letters *OC*,
followed by volume and page numbers.

I should like to express my gratitude to the editors of this series,
Professors J. E. Varey and A. D. Deyermond, for their many helpful comments and suggestions.

1 The Spanish novel in the early twentieth century

1902 is a year of special significance in the history of the Spanish novel. Miguel de Unamuno publishes *Amor y pedagogía*, Pío Baroja publishes *Camino de perfección*, Ramón del Valle-Inclán publishes *Sonata de otoño* and Azorín publishes *La voluntad*. These are works written very early in the literary careers of their authors, and they all evince a fierce determination to offer something entirely different from the then prevalent mode of narrative prose fiction which goes under the general label of nineteenth-century realism.

In the 1890s realism, which in Spain had produced such masterpieces as Galdós's *Fortunata y Jacinta* (1887) and Clarín's *La Regenta* (1885), was in decline. Another doyen of realism, José María de Pereda, also wrote his best works in the 1880s, while Emilia Pardo Bazán, famous for her defence of realism in *La cuestión palpitante* (1883), published her best novel, *Los pazos de Ulloa*, in 1886. The nineteenth-century realist mode is continued into the twentieth century by lesser – though not insignificant – novelists such as Armando Palacio Valdés and Vicente Blasco Ibáñez, but by then the conventional realistic approach had given way in the case of the best writers to a much more complex approach to literature, a change that to some degree even affected the later work of a realist like Galdós.

The demise of realism at the turn of the century has never been fully explained, although it is a general European phenomenon.[1] In general terms realism had accompanied the rise of scientific positivism, with its emphasis on the uncovering of facts. Indeed the literary equivalent of scientific positivism was the naturalism advocated by Emile Zola, according to which the novel, basing itself on a precise study of reality, would attain the status of scientific enquiry. Naturalism was but realism taken a step further, and it

[1] In 1900 Joseph Conrad published his *Lord Jim*, a landmark in the modern English novel. He was soon to be followed by such radical remakers of fiction as Proust, Joyce, Mann, Gide, Kafka and Virginia Woolf.

sustained itself by its claim to follow the systematic and disciplined approach of science. But in the late nineteenth century the enthusiasm for science waned sharply: indeed it is no exaggeration to talk of a widespread collapse of confidence in the ability of science to offer satisfactory explanations of the questions that mattered most to man. The rapid decline of scientific rationalism had a deep impact on the world of the novel. "The very fact that naturalism had declared itself so unequivocally made its position untenable when the scientific substructure collapsed, and quickly led to the discrediting of the realist idea in general in so far as it depended on external philosophical support."[2]

But although the naturalistic brand of realism became rapidly discredited, realism itself was too deeply embedded in Western culture, counting too many great names among its followers – Stendhal, Balzac, Tolstoy – for the idea itself to be denounced. No writer would wish his work to be labelled unreal. What took place at the turn of the century was therefore not an abandonment of realism but its transformation; it was the nineteenth-century approach to fiction that was abandoned, not the idea of realism itself. Thus we find many novelists of the first half of the twentieth century claiming to be realists even though their approach is markedly different from that of nineteenth-century novelists.

It has become fashionable in some quarters to view the work of the new writers at the beginning of the century as a response to social and economic factors, but such an interpretation is incapable of accounting for many of the characteristics of this new literature. The crucial factors were philosophical and artistic rather than social or economic. Nineteenth-century realism was simply a convention of novel writing whose elasticity allowed for different approaches and styles. But it was built on the assumption that there existed an objective reality outside and independent of the work of art which the novelist could aspire in some measure to study and reproduce. Although few nineteenth-century novelists would accept that they were doing nothing more than copying reality, one can at any rate say that realism arose out of a belief in the evident

---

[2] Damian Grant, *Realism*, The Critical Idiom, IX (London, 1970), p. 44. This succinct study is the most lucid exposition I know of the whole question of nineteenth-century realism and its transformation in the twentieth century.

truth of the external world. It is this belief that was questioned
and even rejected at the turn of the century. The philosophy of
Kant, given a new lease of life by Schopenhauer, was revived: objective reality is unknowable since the human mind acts as a filter
imposing its own structures on the objects it perceives through the
senses, thus conditioning our entire knowledge of the external
world. We cannot in point of fact know things directly; we always
and necessarily see things through the distorting mechanism of the
mind. There is no world independent of our senses; what we believe to be objective reality is only subjective reality: I see things
not as they really exist but as my mind tells me they exist. The only
authentic reality therefore is within and not without. Twentieth-
century novelists implicitly, sometimes even explicitly, repudiate
an approach to fiction which is posited on an objective concept of
reality and replace this with an approach in which the reality depicted is seen as the creation of the artist's consciousness. The new
novelists do not reject realism, nor do they reject the world; they
merely reject a realism limited to the material world. They would
claim that they have achieved a more genuine vision of reality:
"What all the moderns have in common – perhaps the only thing
they have in common – is an insistence on the fact that what previous generations had taken for *the world* was only *the world seen
through the spectacles of habit.*"[3]

To understand the nature of the change that occurs in the art
of novel writing at the turn of the century it is vital to recognize
that the course of fiction is altered by a new vision of experience:
the world may still be there, but it is no longer seen with the
same eyes. It is the changing mode of our perception of the world
that lies at the root of the new novel. Twentieth-century novelists
are no longer content to see the novel as a realistic representation
of life – things are no longer as they seem. There is a radical
insecurity in man's perception of the world, and this leads
novelists to question the basis of their art and experiment with
new techniques. For if the novel is no longer a representation
or an exploration of an objective reality, then what is it? For
many writers the newly-found freedom from the – for them –

[3] Gabriel Josipovici, *The World and the Book*, 2nd edition (London, 1973), p. xv.

straitjacket of the nineteenth-century realistic formula is a source not of rejoicing but of anxiety. They have to find a new justification for their art, and this is far from easy, given that "the subjective experience ... is the only objective experience".[4] For if anything I care to write is acceptable, then why write at all? Why is what I write important or meaningful if I could have written a thousand other things instead? Indeed it has been said that "a complete realism is indistinguishable from a complete solipsism, since I am not an object in the world but the limits of my world" (Josipovici, *The World and the Book*, p. 312). But the best writers steer clear of solipsism, that is, of the belief that the self is all one can know, though the surrealists do not always manage to avoid the danger.[5] The problem of the expression of reality is an urgent and pressing one for the twentieth-century novelist, and the technical innovation and experimental unorthodoxy that characterizes the work of almost every major novelist of the Western world in this century is but a search for a formula that will imbue the work with a coherent concept of its own nature, that will justify its existence. The question 'why?' turns into the question 'how?'. How can I as a creative writer best convey to my readers my own concept of the truth, of reality? The message becomes dependent on the medium to such an extent that the two are often indistinguishable, or to put it another way, the novel becomes an exploration of its own possibilities as an art-form. Indeed it is no exaggeration to say that the fictional world becomes more complex and ambiguous than the real one, not only because it is not just a supposed reproduction of a pre-existing reality, but also because it has become a mode of perception rather than an object perceived. A new contract is established between the novelist and the world: reality is still there, but not for the taking; it has to be created, because what counts now is not *what*

[4] Cited by René Wellek in his essay "The Concept of Realism in Literary Scholarship", in *Concepts of Criticism* (New Haven and London, 1963), p. 237.

[5] Surrealism aimed at expressing the subconscious side of man mainly by the use of unusual images and unexpected associations. Just as the naturalism of Zola was the terminal form of nineteenth-century realism, surrealism may be looked upon as the extreme form of early twentieth-century subjectivism. But by and large the novel avoids the surrealist mode.

one sees, but *how* one sees it. Malcolm Bradbury explains it this way:

> The novel – and realism – as Trilling defines these things, do not die out in our century. But they are qualified, and that is a reminder that realism is like reality – that is, not an *absolute*, but a mode of perception, which is subject both to historical change and to subjective interpretation. And novels tend to draw their notions of what is realistic from prevailing and influential views of what orders human experience. (The views of Darwin and the social determinists of early sociological thought lie behind naturalism; the views of Freud and Jung lie behind the realistic psychological novel, the novel of consciousness; the views of Heidegger and Sartre lie behind many of the modern novels which heighten realistic contingency into a philosophy of the absurd.) Certainly the novel does have an inevitable bias towards realism – because it uses the most literal of literary languages, prose; because it tends to emphasise the authenticity of individual and personal experience; because it tends to deal in human relationships; because it does not really have a predetermined form (as tragedy does) but can let the form emerge. But its realism can be expressed so variously that we can speak of realism as a changing attribute of the form, not as a definition of it.[6]

The alleged crisis of the novel in the early part of this century – to which one frequently comes across references in histories of literature – is not a crisis of the novel at all but a crisis of how novels should be written. The whole crucial question of the nature and perception of reality, when transposed into the realm of fictional writing, is subsumed in the problem of form. A new view of reality necessitates a new medium for expressing that view, and the new medium, precisely because it is born out of a new concept of reality, is in turn conditioned by that concept. But the new concept of reality is one that stresses the validity of the individual consciousness, that is, of your or my or anyone's perception of the world. Thus, while a new approach to novel writing is everywhere advocated, there are as many different approaches as there are novelists: Conrad, Faulkner, Gide,

[6] *What is a Novel?* (London, 1969), p. 29.

Hesse, Huxley, Joyce, Kafka, Lawrence, Mann, Sartre, Woolf – each one has his approach to the common problem of 'how shall I write?' Generalizations about the modern novel are therefore fraught with difficulties. But some attempt to understand the new fictional mode is essential if we are to approach Baroja – a product of the new generation of writers – in the right frame of mind. To study the modern novel, or any one of its many representatives, in the very terms of the nineteenth-century novel is to condemn oneself to superficiality and misconception from the start. We must abandon preconceived notions about such typically nineteenth-century values as plot, characterization, storyline, orderly exposition, climax, denouement and so on, if we are to give ourselves a chance of meeting twentieth-century fictional art on its own ground. At this juncture some generalizations are mandatory in order to place Baroja in the context to which he belongs.

Man's conviction that there is a world, Schopenhauer points out, lies within his own consciousness. It can never be proved that objective existence is independent of human cognition. Many twentieth-century novelists, accepting Schopenhauer's view, have come to believe that the only real existence lies within an individual's own consciousness. Events and objects in themselves cease to have any meaning; they are important only in so far as they are perceived by or have an effect upon a consciousness. The novelistic universe is not so much given as perceived by a character. And so it is that in many modern novels the reader finds himself peering all the time, in a manner that can sometimes become quite oppressive, into the consciousness of the central character. The extreme form is to be found in James Joyce's *Ulysses*, where we read the thoughts of the characters even before they have become normal speech. A more common reflection of the notion of seeing reality as the creation of a consciousness can be observed in one of Henry James's favourite techniques, that of using the mind of one character as a "centre of consciousness" through which all events are reflected. James thus renders his story, as he says, "not as my own impersonal account of the affair in hand, but as my account of somebody's impression of it". In general terms it would be true to say that the modern novel deals not with events but with mental states. There is a strong interest in abnormal human types – the eccentric, the schizophrenic, the neurotic, the morbid, the perverse, the idiotic – and even normal beings tend to be seen from a pathological standpoint. Thus the emphasis on consciousness has carried with it a strong interest in personality.

The collapse of confidence in rationalism brings in its trail the abandonment of the idea that human beings behave rationally, or that their behaviour can always be rationally explained. By and large the nineteenth-century novel reflects a stable world, with man in control of that world. Most things were orderly and predictable, including the behaviour of the characters, whose consequentiality has been denounced in this century by André Gide as artificial (in *The Counterfeiters*). The behaviour of characters in the modern novel appears by contrast to be often surprising, inexplicable, contradictory, even pointless. The characters are restless, indecisive, moving from extreme self-assertion to gnawing self-doubt within a short space of time, an enigma to themselves no less than to the reader. At bottom lies the modern interest in personality. The nineteenth-century naturalists had portrayed the individual as being wholly determined by his background: it was the environment that formed personality. Twentieth-century writers on the other hand regard personality as something singular, unique, not so much predetermined as always in the making. The environment is still there, not as a formative influence but as one component of the world observed by the individual consciousness. It is much more a source of disconcertment than of illumination. Baffled and frustrated individuals are a commonplace in the modern novel.

Individual experience in real life is of course a continuing process: it can never be complete; it can end only in the death of that particular individual consciousness. Twentieth-century novelists have tried to reflect this in their work by refusing to present a closed experience in the manner of the nineteenth-century novelist. A climax, a denouement, a well-rounded conclusion to a well-contained action, a resolution of themes, a satisfying end: these conventions come under a mounting attack towards the end of the nineteenth century and they soon give way to quite contrary practices.[7] In the modern novel the flux of consciousness ends in the experience of incompletion; the new way is to present a disturbing, expanding, unfinished experience. This openness of experience is well illustrated by such novels as Gide's *The Counterfeiters*, Kafka's *The Trial* and Mann's *The Magic Mountain*. Life is seen as having no design, simply an open form, an endless process. Within the events of the novel, a protagonist will indeed often attempt to resolve experiences, but usually with no final result. Many twentieth-century novels fail to resolve the problems posed and are left by their authors in a state of irresolvable suspension. This deliberate avoidance of any final resolution in the depiction of an experience is a narrative device intended to reflect a philosophical position: the belief that experience cannot be closed. " 'Might be continued' – these are the words with which I should like to finish *The Counterfeiters*", André Gide writes in his novel.

There can be no statement of completion in a world which is contingent rather than purposeful. The essential contingency of the world, with its concomitant moral and philosophical implications, is one of the major discoveries of the twentieth-century novel in terms of the impact which it has had on technique. Novelists have looked for different ways to order experience, ways which would avoid imposing a logical consistency and a causal relevance on the elements of that experience. For an individual, his existence is given, it is in no way necessary or logical: he simply has to accept the fact that he exists. In Sartre's *La Nausée*, the protagonist, Roquentin, puts it this way:

> The essential thing is contingency. What I mean is that, by definition, existence is not necessity. To exist is simply *to be there*; those who exist appear, *are encountered*, but their exist-ence could never be deduced. There are some people, I think,

[7] "Hardy's sour refusal to make ends meet in his novels, and Conrad's append-ages ('the end such as it is'), are moments in a gradual change in the temper of fiction which is clearly more than temperamental. In the twentieth century, fiction will create a new fable. It will soon be telling its readers that experience is unreduced and irreducible. The novel will soon not only refuse to be 'final', but insist on its right to be not even 'satisfying'" (Alan Friedman, *The Turn of the Novel* [Oxford, 1966], p. 105).

who have understood that; but they have tried to overcome this contingency by inventing a necessary being as their cause. No necessary being, however, can explain existence: contingency is not a mask, an appearance that can be dissipated; it is something that is absolute, and therefore perfectly gratuitous. Everything is gratuitous, those gardens, this town and I myself.[8]

The view of existence as essentially contingent is reflected in the modern novel in the way the author puts his material together. The causally-linked plot, typical of the nineteenth-century novel, was the offspring of the concept of linear causation. By the end of the eighteenth century linear causation became the accepted method of explaining the relationship between sequential events, and it controlled systematic thinking in the physical sciences and in economics, something that can be observed in the new scientific and economic determinism that led in the nineteenth century to Darwinism and Marxism. Correspondingly, novelistic plots were organized according to the principle of linear causation, with the outcome seen as the inexorable result of the working of the machine set in motion by the author. The collapse of faith in scientific rationalism, the conviction that existence cannot be rationally explained, brings with it, in the realm of the novel, a change in the manner of plotting. Tightly-knit, causally-linked plots all but disappear. The emphasis is now on the accidental, the gratuitous, the farcical and even at times the downright absurd. In the search for what is purely contingent, the distinction between what is relevant and irrelevant is almost lost; because relevant or irrelevant to what? Since man is apparently not moving towards an intelligible goal, who can say what is relevant or irrelevant?

But a novel is a created world, and in art at least a world needs a creator, who will in the process of creation impose a pattern on the formless elements that constitute his raw material. Thus, while many twentieth-century novelists may reject the convention of the causally-linked plot where every part fits into another like the cog-wheels in a piece of machinery, they have needed to employ other principles of ordering. These have been

[8] Jean-Paul Sartre, *La Nausée* (Paris, 1938), p. 166.

many. Instead of being held together by a scheme of logical development, many modern narratives have only the continuous
presence of a central character as the source of cohesion. Myth
and symbol as points of reference to guide the reader are also
employed with some frequency. A new concept of time sometimes displaces conventional chronology, giving the novel an
unfamiliar but perceivable pattern. Or there may be an intensi-
fication of the depiction of a character's inner nature, thus afford-
ing the novel a psychological unity. Some authors – Huxley,
Mann, Pérez de Ayala – have even attempted to transpose to the
realm of the novel techniques used in musical composition. Thus,
while many modern novels do not 'tell a story' in the traditional
sense – and we are simply wasting our time if we read *Ulysses*,
To the Lighthouse, *La Peste*, *La Nausée* or a hundred and one
other novels just for the story – they do at any rate offer some
other principle or method of cohesion. Ultimately what has happened as we have moved from the nineteenth- to the twentieth-
century novel is that one set of criteria has been replaced by
another, though the new criteria have turned out to be rather
more complex and difficult than the traditional ones.

The breakdown of the traditional concept of reality as something absolute and unchanging leads to a relativistic view of life
that brings to the novel a wave of experimenting with perspective.
Truth is not absolute but relative to the observer. Many novelists
cease to offer us *the* truth and offer instead the view of a particular mind. The angle from which the narrative is presented
becomes of paramount importance; but the narrative need not
be limited to one angle: many different points of view can be
employed, and this is a technique known as perspectivism, a
technique on which the variations are legion. Joyce's *Ulysses* has
the triple vision of Stephen Daedalus, Bloom and Molly, Durrell's
Alexandria Quartet uses a different perspective for each of the
four constituent novels, Faulkner's trilogy *The Village*, *The
Town* and *The Mansion* shares out the narrative among different
characters none of whom can tell the complete truth of the case
in question, while Virginia Woolf's *The Waves* presents the
interior monologues of six different persons. In these and many
other cases unilateral vision is replaced by a multi-dimensional,

kaleidoscopic approach, and we the readers do not learn *the* truth but only differing versions of it. The technique of perspectivism may be seen as the expression of a world in which nothing seems solid, secure and enduring, a world threatened by a crisis of beliefs in many spheres, moral, social, political, and by the suspicion that one being may be unable to understand another. Just as Einstein taught us that our appreciation of the cosmos and of space and time is relative to our position in the universe, so the modern novelist contends that each individual's view of the world, of society, of other people, is dictated by his own peculiar and unique constitution. Instead of solving the secret of an existence or the behaviour of a character as the traditional novelist was wont to do, the modern novelist prefers to emphasize the mysterious and incomprehensible sides of human existence and the difficulty of meaningful communication between beings. The use of multiple perspectives is one of the most effective tools that the modern novelist can use in order not only to express the insecurity of human perception but also to convey that sense of confusion, of disintegration, of isolation, of alienation in modern man.

The realization that man occupies a marginal and insignificant place in the universe, that seen on a cosmic scale he is nothing but an irrelevance, and that he is at the mercy of forces over which he has no control, has led many writers to adopt an intensely ironic view of the human situation. What is ironic is that one side of man persists in looking for meaning and purpose while another side of him declares that his search is futile. "The metaphysical principle of irony ... resides in the contradictions within our nature and also in the contradictions within the universe or God. The ironic attitude implies that there is in things a basic contradiction, that is to say, from the point of view of our reason, a fundamental and irremediable absurdity."[9] The irresolvable tensions in modern man between reason and emotion, between freedom and discipline, between society and the individual, between the certainty of death and the biological will to live, between the huge increase in scientific knowledge and the realization that we are not one step nearer to providing satisfying

[9] Georges Palante, a French critic, writing in 1906. Cited in D. C. Muecke, *Irony*, The Critical Idiom, XIII (London, 1970), p. 67.

answers to the most basic questions, lead to the adoption of an ironic detachment as a last line of defence. "For him who sees no possibility of reconciling such opposites the only alternative is irony: a sense of irony will not make him any the less a victim of these predicaments but will enable him in some degree to transcend them" (Muecke, p. 77).

But it is not merely man who is trapped; the novelist *qua* artist too is trapped by the constraints of his art. For a novel purports to deal with a truth, a reality. It may be a fiction, but while we are reading it we are asked to treat it 'as if' it were true. Yet a novelist can make his novel seem true only by referring to the world we all recognize. At the same time most twentieth-century writers subscribe to the symbolist view that art is an order beyond and outside life, that it can never be an interpretation of the world. The novelist is landed with an intractable problem: the world of his book can only be the world of his own creative consciousness; yet he aspires to communicate his vision to other beings. This necessity of having to present as in some way an objective truth something that is nothing but an artifice leads in many cases to the novelist viewing his creation ironically, and communicating that irony to the reader by reminding him during the course of his work that he is reading nothing but a verbal invention. This type of ironic novel, common in the twentieth century, though not unknown in the seventeenth and eighteenth, is "literature in which there is a constant dialectic interplay of objectivity and subjectivity, freedom and necessity, the appearance of life and the reality of art, the author immanent in every part of his work as its creative, vivifying principle and transcending his work as its objective 'presenter' " (Muecke, p. 78).

The adoption of an ironic posture on the part of so many modern novelists strongly suggests that there exists a high degree of artistic self-doubt. In exploring a world that he regards as meaningless, the artist may easily come to doubt the meaning and purpose of his art. If life is a deception, then art may be an even greater deception. Life does not make sense to modern man, and yet within the realm of art it is given a type of meaning. The irony of art is that it is gratuitous, an order of beauty and meaning devised by man in a senseless universe. Most great artists aspire to confront their age face to face and to convey its nature and complexities. But an irrational age puts the artist in an impossible position; irrationality cannot be communicated in a verbal constructon except by making it in some way rational. The modern reply to this, if it is a reply at all, is that art is one thing and life another, and each is independent of the other. Nietzsche went further, and in his work *The Will to Power: An Attempted Transvaluation of All Values*, proclaimed that art was of more value than reality: "Art is the great means of making life possible, the great seducer to life, the great stimulus of life."[10] This is echoed by a recent critic who proclaims the "artificiality of the real and the reality of the artificial", and who asserts the "paradoxical notion that we can truly experience life only through art".[11] But such energetic affirmations of the superiority of art over life sound hollow. They fail to dispel the gnawing doubts about the validity of art: in a meaningless universe, can art be anything but meaningless? If he knows not how life functions, can the artist know how art functions? Is the artist's belief in creative art as a means of self-realization a mere illusion that hides the simple fact that his work is but one more useless way of spinning out the tedious thread of time? Nineteenth-century novelists, whatever their shortcomings, had at any rate felt confident about their art and conveyed this confidence to their readers. After the collapse of confidence in rationalism and the abandonment of its novelistic offspring – realism and naturalism – the art of the novel continues to flourish, but it flourishes in an atmosphere of insecurity, disorientation and self-doubt.[12]

In Spain, the novelists who break with the nineteenth-century fictional mode are Unamuno, Valle-Inclán, Baroja, Azorín and

10 Nietzsche, *Complete Works*, edited by Oscar Levy, Vol. XV (London, 1913), p. 290.

11 Robert Scholes, *The Fabulators* (New York and Oxford, 1967), pp. 20–1.

12 The student who wishes to read more on the early twentieth-century novel in general could consult J. Isaacs, *An Assessment of Twentieth Century Literature* (first published London, 1951, reprinted Port Washington, N.Y., 1968). Chapters 3 and 4 are on the novel. Also useful, if of uneven quality, is *Modernism*, edited by Malcolm Bradbury (Harmondsworth, 1976). Chapter 6 contains seven essays on the novel, some of them excellent.

Pérez de Ayala. They have more in common with those European writers mentioned earlier than they have with nineteenth-century Spanish writers. They are moved by the ambition to create a new type of fiction in which the external world will enter as one component rather than as the total substance. In their search for a fresh formula they strip the novel of its objective habits. They introduce philosophical ideas, poetic evocations, and the inner strivings of the self. The renovation of content is accompanied by a renovation of form, with the abandonment of the conventional causal plot and the adoption of techniques the variety of which is subsumed in the all-pervading question of the relationship of an author to his work.

Unamuno's fiction dramatizes his own anguished struggle between mind and heart, and even in those novels where this is not done in an overtly metaphysical framework, the metaphysical implications are nevertheless still there. This is the case of such novels as *Abel Sánchez* and *La tía Tula*, the protagonists of which engage in a search for a personal identity or role in life that will in some way enable them to transcend the limitations and finality of material existence. For Unamuno the novel is an exploration of and a meditation on the spiritual condition of man. But this meditation, to be valuable, to be alive, must be deeply rooted in the writer's self. "Toda novela, toda obra de ficción, todo poema, cuando es vivo es autobiográfico", he declares. Unamuno projects his own problems, preoccupations and anxieties, his own storm-tossed image of himself, in such a way that his works convey a powerful impression of the creative consciousness behind them. His occasional capricious and burlesque insertions, for which he is sometimes criticized, can be seen on one plane as an ironic comment on man's situation and on another as an assertion of the essential irrationality of the artist's task. For if true art is nothing but autobiography, then there is no art.

Unamuno's views on the novel are in several respects strikingly similar to Baroja's. Both of them make the following points: that the plot of the novel ("el argumento") is immaterial; that the creation of existential beings is the important thing; that the polished, well-finished, neatly rounded-off novel is an inferior, lifeless product; that the novel should aspire to be like life itself, "organismo y no mecanismo" in Unamuno's words. It is interesting that both of these writers, whose products are seemingly so different, should appeal to life as the basis of their art and should react against the realistic art of the nineteenth century because they found it too mechanical. Clearly what these writers understand by 'life' in art is not the same as the nineteenth-century writers understood.

Valle-Inclán seems at first to be at the other extreme: that of rejecting life as the basis for art and advocating the beauty of art as an escape from the absurdity of existence. But Valle-Inclán's attitude is nothing like as simple as that. Even his early, 'aesthetic' work reveals an ironic view of the fictional characters and their world, a view that is by extension applicable not only to humanity but even to art itself: the hero of the *Sonatas*, for example, is deliberately made to adopt the pose of famous heroes from romantic fiction, so that the work rather than as an escape into a romantic dream-world can be seen as a parody of it, and therefore since the hero pretends to live in just such a world, as a parody of itself. Valle-Inclán's later work, built around the notion of *esperpentismo*, confirms that his art is much more existential than escapist, aiming at disturbing the reader rather than at providing artistic relief from the burdens of existence. The theory of *esperpentismo* (grotesque deformation) may be obscure and imprecise, but its practice leaves no doubt as to its significance: its distorting vision reflects perhaps better than any other literary phenomenon the breakdown of the traditional view of reality, a reality which it clearly invites the reader to re-assess. Valle-Inclán's novel *Tirano Banderas* is a masterpiece of *esperpentismo* in narrative fiction, in which the traditional unfolding action of narrative prose is replaced by a series of almost static frames each of which captures the characters in an absurd pose.

Fragmentation, incompleteness, suggestiveness, are the hallmarks of the novelesque world of Azorín, a highly personal world where real and fictitious planes meet in a tenuous framework of autobiography. In Azorín the narrative comes as close as possible to being static, as if the confrontation with reality produced a pained passivity in the observer, who can only stare, disconcerted. A marked quality of Azorín's narrative prose is its oscillation be-

tween photographic realism and sudden introspective plunges
that verge on the solipsistic. The nature of the relationship between the inner world of the individual consciousness and the
outer world of material objects is one that preoccupied Azorín
intensely.

Yet another novelist who questions traditional realism in the
novel is Ramón Pérez de Ayala, the most original experimenter
of the Spanish novelists of that period and one who is often compared with Aldous Huxley and André Gide. Pérez de Ayala's
over-riding concern in all his fiction is with perspective: it is a
topic that crops up in every novel and which forms the subject of
one entire work, *Belarmino y Apolonio*. Pérez de Ayala seeks a
formula that will enable the novelist to convey effectively the
sense of the disintegration of an objective reality into multiple
individual viewpoints that is characteristic of the age, but without
destroying the formal unity of a work of art. He wishes, as
novelist, to look at the world with a stereoscopic vision that will
embrace the multiplicity of existing viewpoints. How well he
has succeeded in overcoming what he calls "the original curse of
the novelist" – that is, having to describe reality instead of being
able to apprehend it in three-dimensional vision – is a matter of
opinion, but there is no denying his interest in employing new
techniques to underline our shifting perception of the world
around us. Indeed his interest in perspective is not just a matter
of narrative techniques but is also reflected in his choice of
material: most of Pérez de Ayala's novels involve the transformation of well-known literary themes which are now seen from an
entirely new angle.

The search of these novelists for new forms is symptomatic
of the new age ushered in by the twentieth century, an age in
which a single, uncomplicated view of the universe can no longer
be entertained. The pivot upon which the new art turns is the
fundamental dualism in man: man as an object and man as a
subject; man as a creature living in two worlds, the world outside
him and the world inside him. This acute awareness of the two
dimensions of man brings about a revolutionary change in artistic
perception. The artist is no longer content with observing the
universe but insists on observing himself observing the universe.

The novelistic universe is after all his own creation; it has only the reality given to it by the novelist; "la realidad circundante es una creación del artista", declares Azorín. This leads to the inevitable question: why do I as artist create this particular reality, and what is the relationship between this created reality and me? The novelist has caught himself novelizing. Self-consciousness becomes a characterizing feature to be encountered, to a differing but always significant degree, in all the five Spanish novelists mentioned, a feature which though manifesting itself in many ways is rooted in this fundamental question of the relationship of the creator to his own creation. We shall see how the dialectic creator-creation is at the very core of *El mundo es ansí*.

2 Baroja's development as a novelist up to El mundo es ansí

Together with Unamuno, Valle-Inclán and Antonio Machado, Baroja has passed into literary history as one of the four greatest literary creators that Spain has produced in this century. In Spain to-day he is generally regarded as the most important modern Spanish novelist after Galdós. If this is indeed so then he has been ill-served by scholars and critics, for the amount of serious critical study of his work is paltry in comparison with those of the other 'big three'. Baroja has certainly attracted a good deal of critical attention, but this has tended to be shallow and repetitious rather that illuminating, hostile or panegyrical rather than dispassionate, anecdotal and descriptive rather than analytical, concerned with ideologies rather than with art. As a result we know comparatively little of how Baroja functions as an artist, and this leads to a certain amount of puzzlement on the part of teachers and students who have to make something of Baroja without the benefit of informed criticism as a guide. This is well illustrated by the following passage from a recent and distinguished work of literary historiography:

> The reader of a typical Barojan novel has to abandon many of the principles by which he is accustomed to judge the excellence of prose fiction. The most important habit that has to be unlearnt is that of supposing that close reading of a novel, paying careful attention to the way things are said, will give a better understanding of its meaning and purpose than will a rapid and superficial perusal. The common idea that in a serious novel the characters and events are bound to signify something beyond their immediate relevance to the continuation of the narrative, and the common novelistic practice of using symbolic or allusive imagery in order to give body and feeling to the author's vision, are best forgotten when reading Baroja. Where such features exist, they seem to have crept in by accident, unknown to the author.[13]

[13] G. G. Brown, *A Literary History of Spain*, edited by R. O. Jones. *The Twentieth Century* (London, 1972), p. 33.

Can this view of Baroja be reconciled with his alleged stature as
a novelist? Has Baroja perhaps been over-valued? Or is he more
a victim of his critics' inadequacies than of his own? His fellow-
writers Unamuno, Valle-Inclán and Machado have only relatively
recently been the object of critical study of real distinction, and
there are now signs that the quality of Baroja criticism is im-
proving, so that we may hope to achieve a deeper understanding
of his art than we have at present. In any case, and whatever
the rights or wrongs of the view expressed in the passage just
quoted, my own approach here will be informed by precisely the
opposite belief: that a close reading of Baroja is absolutely essential if we are to identify and understand those significant features
which, far from being accidental, have been consciously and
deliberately included by the author as part of an overall pattern
of meaning. Sixty years ago Ortega y Gasset declared that "Baroja
es, entre los escritores de nuestro tiempo, el menos comprendido,
tal vez por ser el que mayor actividad exige a sus lectores". Ortega
clearly did not think that a rapid and superficial perusal was what
Baroja's novels required. And Ortega was not only a very perceptive critic but also an intimate friend of Baroja's, well acquainted
with the latter's work and artistic preoccupations, so perhaps it is
as well to bear his words in mind.

The first difficulty the student of Baroja faces is the vastness
and diversity of his output. Baroja's sixty-six novels evince such
a variety of approaches that they defy generalized description of
his work as a whole. He wrote adventure novels, philosophical
novels, social novels, historical novels, poetic novels, psychological
novels, dramatic novels, novels with complex plots and novels
with no plots, novels full of description and novels without description, novels in dialogue form and novels bereft of dialogue,
novels with a protagonist and novels without a protagonist. If we
turn to his many writings on the subject of the novel we find that
they do not permit us, any more than the novels themselves do,
to pin down his concept of the art of fiction. His declared aesthetic
theory can be reduced to the proposition that art should have a
human value, a laudable sentiment no doubt, but an impossibly
vague one. A corollary to this is his belief that a writer needs
"el trampolín de la realidad para dar saltos maravillosos en el

aire" (*OC*, IV, p. 320). Imagination and reality, and the interplay between them, are thus the cornerstones of Baroja's novelistic art, just as they are of the art of most great novelists of any age. And even this undogmatic formula hides wide fluctuations, for a few of Baroja's novels are anodyne in their attachment to vulgar, everyday reality, while others are excessively novelesque.

The legitimate generalizations that can be made about Baroja's art as a whole are few, but three aspects which are of importance will be mentioned here. The first point that needs to be made is that Baroja's method is a very fluid one, and we encounter frequent changes in his approach as we move from novel to novel. There is certainly in all his work the indelible imprint of a strong mind with a particular vision of man and life, but there is no sustained application of a particular formula. Baroja himself realized this: "Un oficio en el cual no se emplea el metro es un oficio sin exactitud y sin seguridad. Ahora hay que reconocer que el oficio de novelista no tiene metro" (*OC*, IV, p. 324). This, then, is the first characteristic of Baroja the writer: his artistic eclecticism, his lack of a single, sustained aesthetic of the novel.

Baroja's versatility – his frequent changes of theme and technique – and his theoretical writings, with their endless insistence that there is no one particular technique in novel-writing, are strongly indicative of a fundamental insecurity about the nature of his art. To some extent this is true of most writers of the time and is of course due to their break with tradition and to their attempts at expressing a new view of existence. But Baroja was perhaps the most insecure writer of them all. When he writes about his art he is a mass of contradictions: he advocates a human art, yet he admits that "la novela es quizá lo que no debe ser como la vida" (*OC*, IV, p. 317); he believes that a writer has to search for truth, yet confesses that "he mirado también la literatura como juego" (*OC*, IV, p. 308); he reduces his art to the formula of imagination-rooted-in-reality, but then goes on to acknowledge that "no sé si puedo llamarme realista . . ., no sé lo que es la realidad" (*OC*, V, p. 414).

Anguished self-doubt is the second, and perhaps the dominant, characteristic of Baroja the artist, a characteristic that he infuses into the life of many of his characters, with their constant searchings, self-analyses and instability. Baroja is unsure of his role as a writer, of what he should write about and of how he should write it. His entire production is a sustained search for a more meaningful art. This is apparent not only in the tacit admission in his writings on the novel that he never found the right technique,[14] but also in the disparity both of subject-matter and of technique between novels. One cannot explain the existence of such disparate works as *Zalacaín el aventurero*, *El árbol de la ciencia* and *El nocturno del hermano Beltrán* — to name but three — unless one ascribes to the author a conscious desire to experiment and explore the possibilities of his art. There is also one other peculiar habit of Baroja that supports this view of him as a writer struggling with his art, and that is his use of the prologue as a justificatory or advisory device: in quite a number of novels the reader is confronted with a prologue which purports to tell him something, usually in an ironic, lighthearted or devious way, of the work he is about to read. Indeed Baroja seems to have been not just preoccupied with the question of how novels are written but veritably obsessed by it. When reading him it is sometimes difficult to avoid the suspicion that he is talking a secret language, and that when he writes about his characters and their problems he is cryptically referring to his role as a writer and to his struggles with his art.

The third major characteristic of Baroja the novelist is irony.[15] Right from his very first book, the collection of short stories entitled *Vidas sombrías* (1900), the ironic comment, the mocking tone, the taste for paradox, make their presence felt and will continue to do so to the very end of his career as a novelist. There is irony, too, in Baroja's attitude towards many of his characters, an attitude often characterized by a curious game of association-

---

[14] That he was preoccupied with the technique of the novel is explicitly stated by him, though the specific nature of this preoccupation is not explained: "Yo, desde hace tiempo, me hallo preocupado con esa técnica, no precisamente con la general, sino con la mía propia, y con la posibilidad de modificarla y de perfeccionarla" (*OC*, IV, p. 308).

[15] As with other aspects of Baroja, the existence of irony in his work has occasionally been acknowledged but hardly studied. The best critical study of this subject is in Hugh Probyn's unpublished M.Phil. thesis "Pío Baroja: Aspects of the Development of his Work 1900–1912" (University of Leeds, 1976).

dissociation between author and protagonist in which authorial
involvement with the character is cut short by the adoption of a
posture of ironic detachment; there is irony in the way small
events happen or turn out in the novels; and there is irony in
many of the titles Baroja gives to his novels. So all-pervading is
the presence of irony in his work, that it could be reckoned to be
one of the few fundamental principles of his art. Beneath his inclination to irony there lies an acute preoccupation with the
apparently dualistic nature of reality, more specifically with the
discrepancy between what one is conditioned to think and what
one sometimes discovers, between one's intentions and the intentions other people ascribe to one, between one's intrinsic worth
and one's position in society, between the goodness of a person's
moral code and the inefficacy of his actions or vice-versa. This
type of ironic contrast is extremely frequent in Baroja and stems
not just from the philosophical view of man as a cosmic victim –
he thinks he is in control but he is not – but also from the idea
that man's own social world is based on contradiction and delu-
sion: the ideals which we like to ascribe to ourselves as individuals, justice, love, probity, sincerity, magnanimity, self-
sacrifice, are inoperative within the social structure. But there is
also a less obvious type of irony in Baroja, for his ironic view of
man and society encompasses the artist too. At times he erects
an ironic membrane between himself and his work, he creates an
ironic distance as he looks down half-mockingly at his own
created world, as if to imply that this world is no more than a
pretence. In a world built of subjective interpretations – and for
Baroja as for many of his contemporaries objectivity is a fraud –
confidence about its general validity is likely to wane, particularly
when the artist realizes that his world is limited by his personality.
Indeed there may come a point when the artist doubts the image
which his own work projects of himself. "Cuando el hombre se
mira mucho a sí mismo llega a no saber cuál es su cara y cuál
su careta" (*OC*, V, p. 158), says Baroja, though the words could
just as easily have been written by Unamuno, Azorín or Valle-
Inclán.

El mundo es ansí, published in 1912, is generally regarded as
closing the first phase of Baroja the novelist, a phase which began

in 1900. After *El mundo es así*, between 1912 and 1930, Baroja
was to devote himself almost exclusively to a long series of historical novels which deal with aspects of Spain during the first
half of the nineteenth century. The eighteen novels of the first
twelve years of Baroja's career as a novelist all have either a later
nineteenth-century setting or, as in a majority of cases, a fully
contemporary one.

Baroja's first novel, *La casa de Aizgorri* (1900), is a little
unusual in that it is in dialogue form (conceived originally as a
play), but is more conventional in its use of a strongly dramatic
plot based on social confrontation, with clearly implied good and
evil factions, and with a carefully built-in love interest. The next
novel, *Aventuras, inventos y mixtificaciones de Silvestre Paradox*
(1901), is totally different: a plotless, unpredictable, humorous
tale of an extravagant and eccentric character, punctuated with
brief but telling observations on contemporary society. Five years
later Baroja used the same eccentric protagonist in *Paradox, rey*, a
strange and farcical tale of adventure the real aim of which is to
satirize European civilization, and which is not far removed from
the *esperpentos* which Valle-Inclán was later to create. Baroja's
third novel, *Camino de perfección* (1902), generally regarded as
an early masterpiece, is anything but humorous: here we meet
for the first time the anguished hero of the twentieth century
searching for some meaningful belief, relationship or goal in a
world which he sees as alien, hostile and incomprehensible. For
this novel Baroja adopts the simple quest pattern of primitive
epic narrative, but in his next novel, *El mayorazgo de Labraz*
(1903), he makes use of a much more novelesque, even romantic,
type of plot; yet he also adopts an ironic stance which is noticeable
in his use of paradox in both characterization and plotting, in the
unconventional, unexpected and even aesthetically jarring ending
(the complex and dramatic plot is left open), and more obviously
in the way that, through a gentle and humorous parody of the
traditional device of a source for the tale, he actually emphasizes
its purely fantastic nature.

The next three novels to appear are those of the trilogy *La
lucha por la vida* (1904–5), one of Baroja's most famous works
and one of the most intensely realistic. Here he appears to sub-

ordinate the work of the imagination to the detailed observation
of a concrete, external and identifiable reality, that of the under-
world of Madrid. But the 'life-in-the-raw' approach hides a good
deal of conscious contrivance and of the most deliberate kind of
selectivity, and the occasional ironic intrusions of the author
rather imply that Baroja is uncertain as to whether he wants the
reader to take for real life what is after all a literary artifact. That
Baroja likes to use a known, recognizable, real-life setting for a
purely imaginative construction is fully confirmed by his next
novel, *La feria de los discretos* (1905), in which the realistic and
faithful description of the city of Córdoba, its inhabitants and its
atmosphere is counter-balanced by a somewhat improbable tale
of adventure and intrigue which reads suspiciously like a skit on
Dumas and other nineteenth-century romancers. In his next
novel, *Los últimos románticos* and *Las tragedias grotescas* (a
single work in two volumes [1906–7]), the story-line is emptied
of all drama; its simplicity makes possible the concentration of the
novelist's attention upon the setting itself to such a degree that
it is almost misleading to talk of a setting. The novel is rather
an attempt to capture the atmosphere of Paris and the flavour of
Parisian life, particularly for Spanish emigrés, in the 1860s and
1870s, during the last years of the Second Empire: the novel ends
with the rising of the Paris Commune in 1871. In the evocation of
an atmosphere of decadence, of immorality, of hypocrisy, the
work is supremely successful, but the technique employed consists
neither in grand description nor in naturalist dissection, but rather
in a succession of vignettes which depict impressionistically a
procession of picturesque types from all walks of life. But perhaps
the most significant aspect of this work is in its protagonist,
a gentle and kindly man who discovers to his amazement that he
possesses his own inner reality which is independent of the events
taking place around him and who is thus able to abstract himself
from the sordid behaviour of his own family. At the beginning
of the novel Baroja expresses clearly for the first time an idea
that recurs in his work, namely that events have no meaning in
themselves but acquire significance according to one's reactions to
them: "En lo hondo de nuestro ser, todo el manantial de la
felicidad o de la desgracia proviene de la vida orgánica, del último

resultado, enviado a la conciencia por los sentidos, no de los acontecimientos adversos o felices, sombras sin realidad, ni tampoco de las ideas, que son imágenes esqueléticas de las cosas" (*OC*, I, pp. 811–12).

Baroja seems to have found temporary satisfaction in the formula employed in *Los últimos románticos* and its sequel, for he adopts essentially the same procedures in his next work, again in two volumes, *La dama errante* and *La ciudad de la niebla* (1908–9). The inspiration – though not the principal event – is historical: the attempted assassination of King Alfonso XIII in 1906, and the city of the title is London, to which the heroine and her father, implicated by chance in the attempted murder, are forced to flee. Once more the effort of the novelist is directed towards the apprehension of a deeper reality than the merely physical or external, whether it be that of the city of London or that of the heroine struggling to assert her individuality in a world that in her eyes is demanding submission. To submit is what the protagonist of Baroja's next novel, *Zalacaín el aventurero* (1909), refuses to do. But this novel, though given a precise historical setting, that of the third Carlist war of 1872–4, is an escape from reality rather than an exploration of it: at worst a boyish, action-packed adventure yarn, at best a poetic evocation of Baroja's beloved Basque countryside full of literary reminiscences and mythical allusions, one of several lyrical interludes that occur in Baroja's long novelistic career.

The years 1910–12 see the publication of some of Baroja's best work. The intensity of production of these years, coupled with the problematic nature of both form and content, suggests a conscious experimentation on the part of the author and a preoccupation with certain aspects of his art. More specifically, what seems to be worrying Baroja is the relationship of his central characters to himself. Baroja's novels seem to be getting more and more autobiographical, finding their inspiration in personal reminiscences and experiences, and, what is equally significant, they appear to give a greater insight into the spiritual world of the author. But this turning inwards of the author is accompanied by a tacit or even explicit rejection of what the protagonist stands for. In no other novels (except just possibly *Camino de perfección*) has Baroja been as spiritually close to his protagonists as in the novels of the years 1910–12; yet paradoxically never has he been artistically so far. He wilfully manipulates authorial distance to dissociate himself at intervals from those protagonists into whose anguished lives he appears to be pouring so many of his own ideas, attitudes and anxieties. It is as if he had come to doubt whether a writer could create autonomous characters and objective worlds and to suspect that the characters and the worlds were but projections of the writer. In the novels of this period he seems to be acutely aware that he is studying himself rather than the outside world. Yet Baroja as a person was certainly not an exhibitionist; and he appears to have reacted to the danger of being turned into one by retreating into irony, the clearest technique of which consists in creating for himself a second novelistic persona who will act as a foil to the protagonist.

César o nada (1910), counted among Baroja's half-a-dozen best novels, is a story of political ambition for which he drew heavily on his own experiences as a tourist in Rome and as a Republican candidate in the elections of 1909. The novel is also an analysis of the socio-political situation in rural Spain, and a political programme is put into effect during the course of the book. The use of the author's own experiences as part of the fictional protagonist's experiences, and the attempt to fashion a political ideology, might incline one to read the novel more or less as the author's political manifesto. In point of fact Baroja's technique makes such a straightforward reading quite impossible. The only authorial norm we can infer is that of irony. The writer has created a distance between himself and his protagonist, and this detachment with which he views his character periodically asserts itself in small but significant details of his portrayal. In addition, the story proper is prefaced by a curious prologue in which author meets fictional protagonist and engages in a political argument about issues that will reappear in the novel proper. The original version, published in serial form in a newspaper, also had a highly ironic ending in which the protagonist was finally shown to be a fake. Baroja's ambivalent attitude to his protagonist is further shown by the removal, in the book version, of this rather cruel epilogue and the substitution of an open ending in which no final judgment is passed on the protagonist.

Las inquietudes de Shanti Andía (1911), usually coupled with *Zalacaín el aventurero* as the best examples of Baroja's adventure novels, is more of a book of authorial reminiscences with a sea yarn at its centre. There are reminiscences of Baroja's childhood, of his family and acquaintances, of his native Basque region, and above all reminiscences of a literary kind: *Las inquietudes de Shanti Andía* seems to evoke the memory of his readings of Poe, Mayne Reid, Captain Marryat and Stevenson. The eponymous hero of the novel is not an adventurer at all, but simply the author's narrator-agent, not unlike Conrad's Marlow. Indeed an identification author-protagonist is implied in the opening pages where among other things the narrator calls himself "un tanto novelero". But even Shanti does not seem to provide the necessary shelter behind which the author can safely manipulate his material, and the central part of the tale recedes as other narrators take over (four other characters in addition to the protagonist participate in the narration). There are also periodic shifts in time as the narrative moves from the time of the events to the time of redaction, which itself takes place at different moments, as Shanti himself warns. Again it seems as if Baroja is mirroring in his tale the creative process itself as the author moves back and forth from his real world to his fictional world. At any rate it is obvious that by this time he was incapable of sitting down and simply getting on with telling his story in an uncomplicated, straightforward manner: the preoccupation with the authorial origins of the story and with its narration had become too strong to be suppressed. "El ver mis recuerdos fijados en el papel me daba la impresión de hallarse escritos por otro, y este desdoblamiento de mi persona en narrador y lector me indujo a continuar" (*OC*, II, p. 997), says Shanti, providing a sudden insight into the core of Baroja's aesthetic preoccupation: a narrator is but a reader of himself. It is this limitation which Baroja had been striving to overcome, but which in the final years of his first period, as his novels grow more introverted and autobiographical, threatens to undermine his art.

El árbol de la ciencia (1911), arguably Baroja's greatest novel, is also the most strongly autobiographical one. It is a deeply philosophical and moving story which vividly sums up an entire age and crisis in the history of Western civilization: the collapse of confidence in scientific rationalism at the end of the nineteenth century. But this for Baroja was not just a cultural phenomenon: it was a highly personal matter as well. He was a scientist by training and by inclination, but he was a failed scientist. Baroja had graduated in medicine, had done research for a doctorate, and had practised as a physician but only for a limited period. He never offered any very clear reasons for abandoning his medical career, but temperamental unsuitability and a lack of faith in his own profession had a great deal to do with it. Both his scientific inclinations and his eventual recognition of the limitations of the scientific view of life are novelized in *El árbol de la ciencia*. The experiences of Andrés Hurtado as a medical student and later as a young doctor were Baroja's own experiences; his hopes, ideals and anxieties must have been to some degree Baroja's hopes, ideals and anxieties, and his frustrations and disillusions Baroja's frustrations and disillusions.[16] Hurtado's suicide at the end of the novel, though not brought about by purely philosophical reasons, comes nevertheless immediately after his realization that science has failed to save his wife and child when nature might have succeeded, and thus symbolizes the failure of the scientific outlook on life that the protagonist has so ardently defended during the course of the novel. The closing words of the book, "había en él algo de precursor", are obscure, and could contain an oblique reference to Baroja himself. But Baroja is not content to write about himself in the guise of a fictional character: at certain points he abandons the subjective identification with his protagonist and adopts an external, objective viewpoint. The *desdoblamiento* which Shanti Andía speaks of as he sees himself objectivized in the pages he has written occurs here as well. This time Baroja's technique consists in creating a second character to whom the protagonist can expound his scientific philosophy of life but who picks holes in his arguments and who puts forward a counter-philosophy based on traditional utilitarianism which seems ultimately to be the more correct. Though their philosophies are incompatible, the two characters are not antagonists; indeed there is a bond of mutual respect and understanding be-

---

[16] He said rather curtly that he had included in this novel "mis preocupaciones de médico" (*OC*, VII, p. 800).

tween them. Neither of them on his own can be taken as the author's mouthpiece; but together they represent an authorial conflict. Looked upon as a statement of Baroja's own philosophy, *El árbol de la ciencia* is insurmountably ambiguous, for if a philosophy is built up, it is also pulled down. All of which of course goes to make of Baroja a contradictory but deeply human writer, caught in the turmoil of his own doubts and disorientation, his search for truth frustrated by the limitations of his own mind and feelings, hope countered by despondency and protest by resignation.

By the time of *El mundo es ansí* Baroja's preoccupation with his art had reached the point of obsession, but he was no nearer to answering his own question. And the question was whether his novels were truly studies of the outside world – as he liked to think and more than once declared – or whether they were merely studies of himself. Could a writer create autonomous characters and objective worlds, or should he face the truth that those characters and those worlds were merely projections of himself? *La lucha por la vida* had stood for an art that looked outward, an art in which the writer recognized the forces at work within society and within the world and struggled to incorporate them in his own imaginative vision. But the personal nature of this very struggle could in turn become the art itself. Comparing the novels of 1910–12 with *La lucha por la vida*, it is easy to see that Baroja has become more introverted, more self-conscious, less certain what he is about. His novels are threatening to become studies of the artist's self; in some respects Baroja is getting close to the threshold where art ceases to be art and becomes a purely personal document. Baroja appears to accept, yet at the same time does his best to transcend, what for many writers is an inescapable constraint upon artistic creation: that the artist's quarry is ultimately himself. Baroja's efforts are thus frantically directed towards giving an appearance of objectivity to what is an intensely subjective world. It is this oscillation between subjectivity and objectivity which gives rise to a paradox in Baroja: the more autobiographical the novel, the more difficult it is to infer the authorial norms. The closer the protagonist moves to the author, the farther the author appears to the reader. It is in his more markedly autobiographical novels that Baroja appears to be at his most reticent and ambiguous. He was so intensely affected by the problem of pouring himself into his work that already during or even before the redaction of *El mundo es ansí* he had decided to abandon the problematic subjectivity of his recent novels and branch off into a more objective and less agonizing form: the historical novel. *El mundo es ansí* was to be the last novel of Baroja's artistic crisis, but it was to be the most problematic of all. Up to now the problem had revolved around the question of whether Baroja was writing about himself or about the world outside, or indeed whether he could do both at the same time. *El mundo es ansí* goes further, and is about that very problem itself.

3 El mundo es ansí: *ideology of the work*. *The protagonist*

Like the novels immediately preceding it, *El mundo es ansí* contains a great deal of material taken straight out of Baroja's own experiences and converted into the experiences of the fictional protagonist. His visit to Switzerland in 1907 and his stay in Florence in that same year provided useful material for establishing the settings of the novel.[17] So much so, that when Baroja came to write his book of essays on Italy, *Ciudades de Italia*, in 1949, he felt no compunction about copying numerous passages from Part II of *El mundo es ansí* almost verbatim:

El mundo es ansí

Esta mañana he salido un momento sola a contemplar Florencia. Toda la noche ha llovido abundantemente; el Arno corre turbio, amarillo; el campo está empapado de agua; una bruma ligera empaña el aire. En las colinas del Belvedere y de San Miniato los árboles brillan con un verde húmedo y obscuro; sobre ellos se destacan con un color delicado los grupos de adelfas en flor. En el cielo, gris y muy luminoso, veo como se perfilan, con una línea muy clara, los contornos de las colinas cercanas, con sus iglesias, sus torreones y sus cipreses. El deseo de pasear sola me impulsa a alejarme de la ciudad. He salido a un descampado, dejando a la derecha la calle que se llama de la Cuesta Scarpuccia, y he pasado por debajo de un arco donde hay un prosaico fielato de consumos. Me encuentro al pie de un cerro, a cuya cumbre sube en espiral un camino y en línea recta una escalera larga con varios rellanos. A un lado hay una fila de altos y obscuros cipreses. Esta fila de cipreses, que avanza trepando por el montecillo, hace un efecto de procesión formada por frailes sombríos y tristes. (p. 104)

Ciudades de Italia

Esta mañana he salido para echar un vistazo al pueblo. Toda la noche ha estado lloviendo; el río Arno está turbio, amarillo; el aire, empañado por la bruma. En las colinas del Belvedere y de

[17] See Shaw (*11*, pp. 16–17) for further details.

San Miniato los árboles tienen un verde profundo que mancha a trechos con una nota delicada los grupos esféricos de adelfas en flor. En el cielo gris se destacan con una línea muy neta los contornos de los cerros cercanos con sus iglesias, sus torreones y sus cipreses. He sentido hoy, en este ambiente húmedo, el deseo de alejarme un poco de la ciudad; he atravesado el río por un puente, he salido a una plaza y he tomado a la izquierda, dejando a la derecha una calle que se llama de la Costa Scarpucia. Pasando un arco donde hay una oficina de consumos, se encuentra uno al pie de una colina a cuya cumbre suben avenidas en espiral, y en línea recta una escalera, larga, derecha, que tiene a un lado una fila de altos y oscuros cipreses, que avanza trepando por el montecillo. Esta hilera de cipreses que sube recta hace un efecto extraño. Se diría una procesión de frailes sombríos y tristes. (*OC*, VIII, p. 715)

There are many other passages which coincide substantially and which show that, despite appreciable differences in style, Baroja is borrowing from the earlier work not just facts but also impressions, and that these impressions can be ascribed just as easily to a fictional creation as to the writer himself. The coincidence of material cannot be taken as proof that *El mundo es ansí* is factual; if anything it proves that *Ciudades de Italia* is not.[18] At any rate the comparison between the two works serves to illustrate Baroja's reluctance to distinguish between what he experiences as an ordinary person and what he invents as a writer. The problem here is that the common ground in the lives of protagonist and author naturally encourages us to see also a link in the sphere of personality or ideology, a link which need not necessarily be there. Most of the commentators of *El mundo es ansí* have seen Sacha as sharing the outlook and ideology of Baroja himself. For some, Sacha is little more than Baroja's fictional alter-ego (e.g. 6, p. 177); for others Sacha is the embodiment of a particular thesis

---

[18] Actually Baroja takes great care not to say that it *is* factual (though parts of it clearly are) and, explaining that the work was commissioned by his publisher, he more or less admits that it is patch-work. Several other novels (notably *César o nada*) have been plundered in the confection of *Ciudades de Italia* and the novelesque borrowings have been included without proper adaptation to a non-novelesque context. This is not really surprising: in 1949 Baroja is 76 and his imaginative faculties have suffered a severe decline.

or world-view. The latter interpretation has been clearly and forcefully defended by D. L. Shaw in the critical essay that accompanies his edition of the novel. I quote a relevant passage:

> *El mundo es ansí* is explicitly a thesis-novel. But unlike those of Pereda and Galdós its theme is not that of a specific social problem: it is in a sense that of the *Bildungsroman*: human nature in general. The description of Sacha's acquisition of insight has a dual purpose. Through her experiences with others it reveals the preponderant role in personal relationships played by instinctive selfishness and ignobility, that "maldad pasiva, torpe, que nace del fondo del animal humano, una maldad que casi no es maldad", which Baroja believed was an integral part of human nature. At the same time through her own actions, it emphasises the difficulty, even for those who possess a measure of natural disinterestedness and idealism, of avoiding the pitfalls of illusion and of recognising in one another their only source of comfort and protection against the rest. The narrative, conditioned as it is by Sacha's development, follows a brief rising curve with its peak in Sacha's first marriage, covering her early phase of political and emotional illusion. This is followed by a gradually falling sequence of events, interrupted only briefly by her marriage to Velasco. Her realisation at Navaridas that *el mundo es ansí* is confirmed by the collapse of her second marriage and by her failure to perceive in Arcelu a potential support. This failure, together with her discovery on returning to Russia that revolutionary idealism has vanished, completes the pattern, adding a note of irony to the pathos and bitterness of the book's ending. (*11*, p. 18)

For Shaw, then, the phrase "el mundo es ansí" is a pointer to the thesis, though only of course *a posteriori*, in the light of what happens. For it stands to reason that, in a thesis novel, the message will be as convincing or as unconvincing as the characters and the events allow, since it is through them that the author has to drive home his message or illustrate his idea. Obvious manipulation of character and events to fit the thesis will inevitably tend to detract from the message: if the narrative becomes recognizably tendentious the reader is more likely to resist persuasion. If *El mundo es ansí* is read as a thesis novel one has to admit, I think, that the thesis is upheld by exceedingly obvious and artificial means. The protagonist is too idealistic, her first husband is too materialistic, her second husband too callous, her experiences too exclusively negative, her victimization at the hands of the cruel world too conspicuous and her discovery of the motto on the shield at Navaridas rather too convenient. The sense of artificial arrangement is so marked that the philosophical message is impaired. But on the other hand the apparently obvious inclusion of a message should be a warning that this interpretation could be too simple and ready-made and that there might be more to *El mundo es ansí*.

Also worth considering is the nature of the message itself. Is the thesis an original, or valuable, or challenging, or even controversial one? Does it provide some new insight into the human situation, or into a particular social, political or historical situation? After all, if a novelist is going to write a serious novel about a particular idea or a particular ideology, one would expect – or even demand – that the idea or the ideology should be of sufficient value to admit of discussion and consideration. Is this the case with *El mundo es ansí*? My own view is that it is not. If *El mundo es ansí* is a thesis novel, the thesis presumably can only be that human beings tend to be selfish and insensitive – at best blind to the feelings of others, at worst downright callous; goodness is an illusion, reality is evil. Quite apart from whether this view of human nature is correct or not, as an idea it is so trite that it scarcely justifies calling it a thesis. Indeed it seems hardly worthwhile writing a novel to illustrate such a message. It may well be that the protagonist of *El mundo es ansí* does discover that she too has been cruel, as she feels others have been cruel to her, but the protagonist's attitude is not necessarily the author's, nor need it follow that the real message of the novel is to be found purely and simply in her discoveries. As I explained in the previous chapter, the relationship author-protagonist in earlier Barojan novels was not simple and stable but complex and shifting, and it may well turn out to be the case that in *El mundo es ansí* the author does not fully identify himself with the protagonist's discoveries about the world and about herself.

Moreover, the phrase "el mundo es ansí" need not necessarily be taken literally; the title of a book does not by itself constitute a reliable indication of the way the content should be taken. The titles of Baroja's novels cannot invariably be taken as literal pointers to the meaning: in *El árbol de la ciencia* the philosophy contained in the title is the one that in the novel is defeated rather than upheld; in *Las inquietudes de Shanti Andía* Shanti turns out to be a sedentary and contemplative individual; in *Camino de perfección* and *La feria de los discretos* the titles are decidedly ironic. If "el mundo es ansí" is to be taken as a simple and straightforward statement of ideology on the part of the author, other internal evidence from the novel would need to be adduced, although the same applies of course – in greater measure if anything – to an interpretation which seeks to deny this. At the root of the problem lies the whole question of the character and development of the protagonist herself and how she has been depicted by the novelist. D. L. Shaw sees the life of the protagonist as a journey of self-discovery which depicts Sacha's gradual acquisition of insight with the destruction of her illusions and the realization of what life is really like. I believe that a rather different view of Sacha is possible, a view which I hope will emerge as I analyse her character, and one which has deep implications for the interpretation of the novel as a whole.

Having read the later works of Tolstoy and become infused with the apostolic ideal of raising the wretched existence of the Russian peasants to a level of moral and spiritual awareness, Sacha discovers, predictably but for her unexpectedly, that the peasants would not listen to appeals for either ethical perfection or improvements in hygiene: "Sacha quedó horrorizada al medir el abismo de la brutalidad del pueblo ..." (p. 53). There is of course nothing wrong with Sacha's ideals; what is wrong is that her attitude completely fails to take into account the reality of the situation. It is only the prudent measures taken by her father that save her from imprisonment or exile after the uprising of 1905. In Geneva Sacha and her friend Vera form a Quixote-Sancho contrast. Vera has too much good sense to be persuaded by Sacha's idealistic ambitions of self-sacrifice in the cause of peasant reform: "Vera, con su buen sentido, no se convencía" (p. 58). Sacha, on the other hand, regards her friend's purely feminine interests with an air of amused superiority: "Sacha se

reía de las ingenuidades de su amiguita" (p. 60). Sacha's confusion between ideas and feelings, which is a quality of her
character that will persist to the end, is already becoming
apparent. She reacts with pained indignation when Leskoff asserts
that the fair sex is temperamentally ill-suited to work in the
scientific, political and artistic spheres: "La idea sustentada por
Leskoff acerca de las mujeres indignaba a Sacha. Ni su amabili-
dad, ni su simpatía por ella eran bastante para hacerle olvidar
aquella opinión, poco halagüeña, acerca del sexo débil" (p. 64).
But the fact is that Sacha herself is inclined this way, even though
she is reluctant to recognize it: "Sacha comenzaba a creer que su
superioridad científica le costaba demasiados trabajos y se le iba
atragantando y haciendo un tanto desagradable ... Sacha com-
prendía que este concepto [de la ciencia por la ciencia] no eran de
esos que pueden encarnar en un temperamento de mujer y lo
aceptaba con muy poco entusiasmo" (p. 64). The root of the
problem lies in the intellectual posture that Sacha adopts and
which prevents her from coming to terms with reality:
"[Aquellos estudiantes] a fuerza de leer y no vivir habían perdido
la noción de la realidad, sus ideas provenían de los libros, sin base,
sin comprobación en la vida. Este irrealismo era la característica
general de todos ellos" (p. 60). This bookishness and abstraction
also comes through in Sacha's ecstatic transportation when she
listens to the scheming Klein reciting romantic poetry, and when
she hears a beggar playing a tune on the barrel-organ:

> "Connais-tu le pays
> où fleurit l'oranger?

y Sacha creía encontrarse en un mundo de sueño, en el taller de
algún viejo artífice de la Edad Media" (p. 74). Sacha's flight
from life into art is such a central aspect of her character, and
hence of the book, that I shall return to this point at greater
length later in the analysis.

Sacha believes herself to be a revolutionary socialist ("creía
serlo" are the words of the narrator), and this prevents her from
seeing through the sham socialism of Klein, who is merely trying
to impress her. Sacha has no real feelings for Klein. Her affair
with him has neither passion nor conviction; it is mere senti-

mental self-indulgence: "Si el aumento de la energía humana es la característica de la pasión, ella podía dudar de sentirla; pero si el amor es melancolía, dulzura, tristeza nostálgica, entonces sí estaba enamorada" (p. 86). Sacha is in love with love; she lives in a dream-world, where feeling is an aesthetic rather than an emotional experience. This aspect of Sacha was obviously considered crucial by Baroja, since he comes back to it again and again:

> Ernesto, que comprendía las vacilaciones de su novia, la empujaba hábilmente por el camino del romanticismo. Klein se las echaba de bohemio, de hombre a quien no preocupa el día de mañana, y Sacha no notaba la mixtificación. Muchas tardes de buen tiempo tomaban los dos un bote e iban a pasear por el lago. Aquella decoración espléndida influía fuertemente en Sacha. A lo lejos, el monte Blanco aparecía como una inmensa cantera de mármol, los barcos pasaban con sus grandes velas triangulares; cerca de los muelles, los cisnes iban en bandadas, y al pie de los pilares de los puentes se reunían flotando las gaviotas.
> Sacha se dejaba llevar por el encanto de la Naturaleza y por el encanto de las palabras. (p. 87)

Incapable of experiencing deep emotion herself, Sacha is astonished when she discovers the intensity of her friend Vera's infatuation with Semenevski. Sacha is at bottom an aesthete, making up for her emotional shallowness by cultivating a sensitivity for nature and for words. She thinks that she will eventually fall in love passionately with Klein; but instead she finds the honeymoon something of a let-down. Literature had given her false expectations, and Sacha, as the narrator tells us, "tenía la mentalidad formada por la literatura" (p. 96). She now begins to doubt whether Klein was the right choice and whether Leskoff might not after all be right about the man who is now her husband. The rupture, with the attempted murder of Klein by Sacha, comes about as a result of Klein's extreme discomfiture in Russia and Sacha's attachment to her native land. It is the difference between their respective attitudes towards the country and the race that sparks off the quarrel that soon develops into mutual hostility and contempt. Yet curiously enough, as soon

as the divorce comes through, Sacha seems to forget her attachment to Russia and decides to leave Moscow and settle in
Florence.

No sooner has she arrived in Florence than she begins to hanker
nostalgically for Moscow and for the protected world of her childhood: "Mi querida Vera, hacemos muy mal en salir de nuestro
país, en perdernos en lejanas tierras" (p. 109). Despite her dis-
claimers about art in her letters to Vera, Sacha indulges in artistic
pursuits. Similarly, though her advice to Vera may be sound, she
herself is incapable of avoiding the pitfalls she outlines: "¿quién
te asegura que una nueva pasión no ha de brotar entre las cenizas
de la antigua? ¿Quién te dice que no vas a depositar tu nueva
pasión en una persona baja, egoísta, vulgar, que no sólo te haga
sufrir, sino que te avergüence y te envilezca?" (p. 117). This is
what is about to happen to Sacha herself for the second time.
Earlier she had rejected Leskoff in favour of Klein; now she rejects the Hungarian painter Dulachska in favour of Juan de
Velasco. Sacha's mistake, once again, is that she decides with her
mind instead of with her heart. Klein had been preferred to
Leskoff because his ideology was more acceptable to Sacha. But
Sacha had soon discovered this ideology to be a mere façade:
Klein was really a shallow and vulgar individual; and later, in a
letter to Vera, she commends Leskoff for his great spirit and
energy. Having thus decided that these are the qualities which
she had failed to appreciate in Leskoff and failed to find in her
first husband, she now rejects Dulachska as sentimental and
instead accepts Velasco, who is "el polo opuesto del pintor
húngaro en carácter, en ideas y en todo ... Velasco me parece un
hombre que debe tener mucha energía" (p. 123). So this time
it is not poetry that Sacha willingly succumbs to: "ya no era
la poesía del panorama espléndido" (p. 127); this time it is her
willing submission to a dominant personality that leads her into
a fresh marriage. Needless to say, her second choice of a husband
will turn out as unfortunate as her first.

The doubts set in immediately after the wedding: "no veo
claro en mi porvenir" (p. 128), in a situation which is the exact
parallel to that following her first marriage: "Sacha estaba seria
y algo pensativa. El porvenir se presentaba ante ella como una

interrogación" (p. 89). Sacha has learnt nothing from her first marital experience; at the time of her marriage to Velasco she is still as uncertain as ever about herself and about other people. The narrator of the prologue, who meets her at the time of the wedding, finds her childishly naive. But the morbid sentimentality which she displays in her diary is gnawing constantly at her soul and preventing her from a healthy enjoyment of life. This is well brought out by her discovery of the small shield over the doorway of a house in the little town of Navaridas. At the moment when she comes across the shield she has no real cause to feel gloomy or pessimistic. Yet she allows herself to be impressed by this picture of a rather trite symbolism more than by anything else she sees in Spain, and it provokes an outpouring of moody philosophizing and soul-searching. Having persuaded herself, intellectually, that "el mundo es ansí", Sacha will of course have no difficulty in finding confirmation all around her and inside her. Having adopted a certain philosophic posture, she will look for corroboration in her experiences.

Sacha's aestheticism continues to be marked:

> El sol brillaba de una manera mágica; parecía que las piedras y las plantas iban a incendiarse, a fundirse, con la luz del día; yo también tuve un momento de esperanza ilusoria, de creer que bastaba llegar a esta tierra soleada para ser feliz ...
>
> Entre Córdoba y Sevilla el cielo comenzó a llenarse de nubes y el espejismo de mi alma palideció y se borró. (p. 139)

Sacha's life is an unbroken circle of false expectations followed by realization, followed by false expectations, followed by realization ... The only constant is her melancholia, which in her writings she projects onto the landscape:

> Es un hermoso paseo con sus palmeras, sus naranjos y sicomoros, pero me da una gran impresión de tristeza. (p. 146)
>
> Luego por los jardines del Vergel, hemos ido al paseo de la Victoria, un paseo muy hermoso y muy triste. (p. 176)

Beauty and sadness go hand in hand. Sacha reduces life to art and to symbol: "El mundo es ansí. Esta sentencia del escudo de Navaridas se me viene a la imaginación a cada paso" (p. 146).

The break with her second husband comes in a sudden rebel-

lious outburst which once again repeats the experience of her first
marriage. Typically she reaches her decision while absorbed in
contemplation of the moonlight:

> Pasé muchas horas a obscuras delante del balcón viendo como
> brillaba la luna en las aguas de la ría. Vi claramente que me
> había engañado, que debía marcharme.
>   Estaba decidida; tenía el sentimiento de un pueblo que se
> levanta contra el tirano. (p. 181)

She brushes aside Velasco's apology, thus giving the lie to her
own declaration that had he shown signs of repentance she might
have forgiven him, and proceeds to put her plan into action and
abandon Spain. Yet she is still as prone to self-deception as ever:
she believes her return to Russia will dispel her feelings of sadness; but all she finds is "un neuvo espejismo" (p. 182), "un
terrible desencanto" (p. 183). The world she finds is not the
world she dreams of, and all she can do is to take refuge in what
is by now her stock response: "¡El mundo es ansí! Con mucha
frecuencia me acuerdo de aquel escudo del pueblo y de su concisa
leyenda" (p. 183). She soon tires of life in Moscow and goes to
visit her friend Vera in Geneva, but Vera's domestic contentment
and dedication to the practical sides of life are for Sacha a disappointment; she thinks she finds Vera much changed, whereas
Vera of course has not changed at all. Sacha's expectations of
forming a spiritual relationship thus remain unfulfilled, but she
has one more attempt by deviously trying to re-establish contact
with José Ignacio Arcelu. The narrator puts it pointedly: "Como
ni Moscú, ni Ginebra le daban lo que esperaba, escribió a España,
a Margarita Arcelu . . ." (p. 184). But her last hope is dashed to
pieces:

> Al leer esta carta, Sacha se encerró en su cuarto y estuvo
> llorando. Ella también, al hombre que la quería humildemente,
> desinteresadamente, le había tratado con indiferencia y con
> desdén.
>   Y el lema del escudo de Navaridas, le vino otra vez a la
> imaginación: "El mundo es ansí". (p. 184)

But no; it is really Sacha who is *ansí*, and who has been *ansí* all
along. Her naivety in sentimental matters, her mystical expecta-

tions, her inability to judge her own feelings and those of others persist right to the very end. Her letter to the narrator in the prologue, which chronologically takes place some time after the epilogue, once more serves to confirm two basic aspects of her personality. One is her continual self-delusion; referring to her present abode in Switzerland, she confesses: "Me instalé aquí creyendo encontrar paz y reposo para el espíritu, y me equivoqué". The other is her aesthetic posture: "Estos hermosos días de Otoño me llenan de melancolía" (p. 42). The letter to the narrator is flowing with self-pity. All Sacha sees before her is "vivir sin una esperanza"; but this is no new insight; she has said it all before, when shortly after the break-up of her first marriage she had written to Vera in exactly the same terms: "Vive una ya sin esperanza ..." (p. 107).

Sacha's life does show some development, the development of disillusion, the descent into melancholia and self-pity, the escape into an unreal world of aesthetic contemplation where the individual becomes conditioned to a sentimental response by the mere consideration of the weather or the landscape. The fact that Sacha is the protagonist of the novel, or that the reader hears her voice directly in the form of her letters and her diaries, or that she is an essentially good person, must not be allowed to obscure the fundamental aspects of her portrait: she is morbidly sentimental, she is an aesthete, she is addicted to melancholia. She is, in all, a moving but pitiable character, who can scarcely be taken as representative of the world at large. Her portrayal certainly does not suggest that in Sacha Baroja was attempting to sustain the thesis that 'the world is like this'. The world of Sacha may be 'like this', but Baroja makes it amply clear that it is Sacha herself who has forged her own world, and this is where the technique of the novel, which will be discussed in the two succeeding chapters, has an important role to play.

Equally improbable seems to me the idea that the novel is intended to portray Sacha's gradual acquisition of insight, in other words that it can be interpreted as a journey of self-discovery in which Sacha shows increasing awareness of others and can, before the end, see her own past in perspective. For Sacha is still unable to make sound judgments at the end of the book, in the last chapter of Part III, in the very last page of her diary. And the mock-Schopenhauerian dictum of the last two paragraphs of her diary are followed by further errors of judgment in the epilogue and in the letter to the narrator, already referred to. True, that in this letter Sacha shows she has no illusions left; but she is no nearer to understanding herself; nowhere is there any sign of a real insight into the nature of her predicament. Indeed the last news we have of Sacha (chapter III of the prologue) is that she has allowed herself to be parted from her daughter, for whom she had earlier expressed such motherly concern as to feel unable to meet her husband's request for an active social life (p. 146), and the words of the Swiss lady suggest that she is no nearer to solving the problem of her personal relationships.

The Karolyi-Amati episode, which Sacha relates in Part II, might conceivably be construed as evidence that she is gaining in insight and awareness of others, but a close analysis of the episode shows that it provides no convincing proof of this. Sacha does see her suspicions about Amati's intentions towards María confirmed; but she at first admits that she is speculating. She concludes that he is "un vividor y un farsante" (p. 122) only when her maid provides revealing information about the life he leads; after this she can hardly go wrong in her assessment, and no deep insight is needed to realize what Amati's motives are. And on the other hand Sacha is forced to admit that she does not understand María: she cannot tell whether she is feigning or not (p. 120). The whole point of the Amati episode seems to be rather to show Sacha's blindness. She accuses her friend of *estetismo* without recognizing the same quality in herself; she realizes the danger her friend is in but fails to see that she herself is in precisely the same situation. Velasco is not a fortune-hunter ("aventurero") like Amati, Sacha concludes, because he has money to spend (p. 126). And that is the level of Sacha's insight. It seems almost superfluous to add that what Baroja wants to show is Sacha's naivety and immaturity, not a newly-acquired perception into human psychology.

So far I have tried to show that a close reading of the novel offers no real support for an ideological interpretation of the work, whether this is conceived in terms of an illustration of human nature in general or of a journey of self-discovery in particular. While on the question of ideology one further aspect of *El mundo es ansí* deserves to be considered, namely the references to Spain and their function in the novel. Generally speaking the references to Spain in Part III come in one of two forms: either direct from Sacha, or from Arcelu as reported by Sacha. Let me take each of these two cases in turn.

Sacha's diary is written very soon after she has made the acquaintance of the Spanish writer who acts as witness at her wedding, and the latter informs the reader in the prologue that Sacha had very naive ideas about Spain: "La rusa tenía en general ideas absurdas de nuestro país" (p. 39). No doubt these ideas will be modified by experience, but the reader has been warned: Sacha is not to be taken as a reliable authority when she talks about Spain. At first Sacha limits herself to consigning to her diary her impressions of a new country; but after her discovery of the shield at Navaridas, generalizations about Spain, Spaniards and Spanish life begin to creep in among her observations, and these observations, of a censorious kind (pp. 136, 138, 142, 143, 144, 145), not only show the disappointment that Sacha experiences in her adopted country but also, and perhaps more significantly, grow increasingly violent as Sacha feels her marital situation worsening. Her attack on the alleged inconsiderateness of Spanish males (p. 144) is a reflection of her disappointment in her husband; while her over-reaction to a rowdy and typically vulgar Andalusian *flamenco* band, which she describes as "canallesco y desvergonzado ..., cínico y grosero" (p. 145), is her way of protesting at being forced to lead a social life which she finds such a strain. Sacha's comments on Spanish life can hardly be said to amount to a bitter critique: the diary tells us much more about Sacha's personal frustrations than about Spain.[19] Indeed Sacha's views about Spain are so enmeshed with her personality that they are at times contradictory. She refuses to stay in Spain in the company of Arcelu's sisters because "esta vida vegetativa para mí sería impossible" (p. 182), yet later she confesses to her cor-

[19] For the opposite view (i.e. that the diary does contain a bitter critique of Spain) see Shaw (*11*, pp. 20–1).

respondent in the prologue that her mistake was to entertain a hope of finding in Spain "una vida de calma y de tranquilidad" (p. 42). Now that Velasco has been pushed out of her life she can remember Spain with affection, "con cariño, con verdadera simpatía" (p. 42). Sacha's views on Spain are as mixed up as her views on herself and on her life.

With the appearance of Arcelu into the story the comments on Spain are taken over by him. Are his views any more reliable than those of Sacha? Shaw believes that Arcelu is a self-portrait by Baroja (11, p. 26). I have compared the portrait of Arcelu with the portrait Baroja gives of himself in his memoirs, and, with the sole exception of their baldness, I have found nothing in common; on the contrary, there are significant differences. Arcelu is clean-shaven; Baroja had a beard. Arcelu uses a monocle; Baroja did not even wear spectacles. Arcelu smokes; Baroja did not (except occasionally in his old age). Arcelu is tall and thin; Baroja was of medium height and build (on this Baroja is very insistent). Arcelu refers to himself as of Mediteranean stock; Baroja liked to underline his Nordic descent. Arcelu admits that his newspaper articles are hypocritical and that he writes to please; Baroja's newspaper articles and reviews on the other hand were at times so blunt and uncompromising in their denunciations that they frequently got him into trouble and on one occasion they even cost him his job. Finally, Arcelu is described as a man of many talents who could have succeeded in whatever role he would have chosen; Baroja was a failed doctor, a failed business-man and a failed politician. The dilettantism which Sacha ascribes to Arcelu cannot of course be attributed to Baroja with any justice. Once he had found his role in life Baroja stuck to it with commitment and dedication. The creative effort involved in sitting for endless hours alone in a room filling blank pages with words is itself proof enough of the assertion of the will. Baroja was not *abúlico*. And Arcelu is not a self-portrait by Baroja: the author figure in the prologue, when asked by the Swiss lady whether he knows Arcelu, states quite categorically that he does not (p. 44).

Arcelu's portrayal, then, should discourage, rather than encourage, the reader to pin this particular character's ideas about Spain onto Baroja. What about the ideas themselves? Do they add up to a systematic ideology or to a serious critique? The answer can only be an emphatic no. Even a perfunctory reading of the conversations between Sacha and Arcelu will reveal the simple fact that Arcelu's comments are flippant, extravagant, eccentric, or just humorously absurd. Sacha, who whatever her failings in the emotional and sentimental sphere is intellectually no fool, receives them with amused incredulity. His comments during the visit to the art gallery are described by Sacha for what they are: "observaciones cómicas". When he talks about himself Sacha calls him "un farsante" and "un fantaseador". His conversation is "amable y mundana", and its value lies purely in its lighthearted entertainment: "Las observaciones de Arcelu ... a mí me hacen gracia", says Sacha, and Arcelu himself acknowledges his whimsicality: "... me gusta pedantear un poco acerca de la vida y de la sociedad" (p. 162). The ten pages in which Arcelu expounds his fantastic theories about Spanish culture and society are preceded and concluded by references to his garrulous nature: "Arcelu no quiere más que hablar a todo pasto" (p. 162), and, "Y Arcelu sigue hablando sin parar, en una elucubración continua" (p. 172). The ideas themselves are a mixture of perceptive comments, ingenious extemporizing, outrageous explanations and eccentric suppositions. Arcelu's disquisitions bring out his personality very well. He is a dilettante of the spoken word, a mixture of journalistic slickness, sardonic humour, and an ability to captivate intellectual women like Sacha with his easy command of language, his show of knowledge and his original and entertaining observations. His is certainly an engaging personality, but there is not very much of it. He is something of a clown, though Sacha, always inclined to see the pessimistic side of life, detects in him an inward sadness. At any rate it is quite clear that neither Sacha nor Arcelu takes his ideas very seriously; so why should the reader?[20]

Arcelu does of course fulfil a particular function within the novel. As Shaw rightly points out (*11*, p. 21), Arcelu provides

[20] Shaw says that Baroja "allowed himself to take seriously the pseudo-anthropological fantasies outlined in Part III" (*11*, p. 27). This is possible; but it is at least equally possible to interpret the obviously humorous title of chapter XVI as a pointer to the opposite.

a contrast with Velasco's character and with his ideas. But it is also worth considering how this contrast is brought about. Arcelu comes to visit his cousin at the hotel and is invited to lunch by Velasco. During the course of the discussion on painting, Arcelu makes a provocative and flippant remark about this art, a remark to which Velasco, not unnaturally, responds. In the words of Sacha: "La opinión de Arcelu ha producido una verdadera cólera en Juan, que ha acusado a su primo de farsante y de preocupado por parecer original" (p. 149). And yet, immediately afterwards, Velasco expresses an interest in his cousin's lodging and through his own good offices secures Arcelu more comfortable accommodation in his own hotel. It is impossible to reconcile this with Sacha's declaration immediately afterwards that "mi marido siente una profunda antipatía por Arcelu" (p. 153) and with her implied suggestion that he entertains a feeling of hatred towards him (p. 155). By this time Sacha has already begun to turn against her husband. Her first complaints have found their way into her diary just before the appearance of Arcelu. Sacha immediately finds in Arcelu what she misses in her own husband: a solicitous nature. Whereas she feels that her husband neglects her, preferring to lead an active social life, in the case of Arcelu she finds herself the centre of his attentions: "Me alegro de que Arcelu esté en el hotel, porque es un hombre muy amable y muy atento conmigo" (p. 152); "Arcelu está cada día más amable conmigo, tiene una serie de atenciones que me conmueven" (p. 178); and, "¡El buen Arcelu era tan amable para mí!" (p. 180). The fact that Arcelu is dilettantish and mundane, as Sacha is forced to recognize, is of little consequence, given that in him she finds what she desperately hankers for: friendship and communication. From now on Arcelu displaces Velasco in Sacha's diary, and the comparisons which she makes between them are always to the detriment of the latter. Despite the difference in personality between the two men, the antagonism which Sacha sees between them is not supported by any hard facts. It certainly does not prevent them from going off together to the *taberna del Resbalón*. The real antagonism is between Sacha and Velasco. The more intense her feelings of revulsion for Velasco become, the more attractive she finds Arcelu and the more she insists on the differences between the two men. When Velasco starts chasing La Coquinera it is not he but the gentlemanly Arcelu who makes the conquest: "La Coquinera ha hablado con gran respeto con Arcelu, a quien considera por su familia de posición en el Puerto de Santa María, y le ha dicho que se ríe de Juan y de su rival el pintor." All of which gives Sacha the opportunity to comment unfavourably on her husband: "Si lo llegara a saber mi marido, tendría por Arcelu un odio furioso" (p. 173). With the departure of Arcelu, Sacha's loneliness intensifies, and her hostility towards her husband comes out in full flood when he reacts to an anonymous letter by telling his wife to stop seeing Arcelu. Yet again Sacha sees hatred in her husband: "La falsedad de su posición le hacía incomodarse en frío y le hacía volcar su odio secreto contra Arcelu y su familia. En sus palabras había algo feo, que inspiraba repulsión" (p 181). By dint of comparing Velasco with Arcelu Sacha has come to feel revulsion for her husband. Her feelings of loneliness and despair have reached a point where they impair her judgment, and while she expects her husband to dismiss his anonymous letter as false, she quite readily accepts hers as true, forgetting that La Coquinera had already laughed off Velasco's amorous advances. But by this time clear-headedness and impartiality are too much to expect from Sacha. Her over-sensitive nature has reached its limits of endurance and she is in full flight from an unbearable reality. While Arcelu was there he was able to fill the void in her life and make up for the emptiness in her marriage. Now all she has left is her "afán por huir" (p. 182).

There is, I would suggest, no real acquisition of insight on the part of Sacha, though there is, it is true, a process of disillusionment. This process of disillusionment, however, is not necessarily accompanied by a greater self-awareness; on the contrary, Sacha seems to live in a perpetual self-delusion, and her periodical clashes between her expectations and her discoveries fail to shake her out of her over-sensitive and semi-mystical attitude. In the end her illusions are reduced to mere self-pity.

I would submit, therefore, that *El mundo es ansí* is neither a thesis novel nor even a *Bildungsroman*; that is has no ideological message of any kind; and that it is not conceived as a journey of self-discovery. It is the story of a naive intellectual whose emotional confusion prevents her from reconciling herself to reality. Her inability to come to terms with her own sensibilities, to judge correctly her own feelings and those of others, prevents her from establishing or maintaining meaningful relationships with other people and brings about an intense loneliness and isolation, which in turn leads to an escape into the world of words. It is here that I believe the real meaning of *El mundo es ansí* is to be found, for around the verbal outpourings of his fictional protagonist Baroja has spun an intricate yet inconspicuous web of associations and allusions whose significance will become apparent only after an analysis of the novel's narrative structure and technique has been carried out.

There is nothing casual about the narrative method of *El mundo es ansí*. The techniques employed by Baroja in telling the story of Sacha Savarof are deliberate and crucial. During the course of this chapter I shall study the general structure and narrative disposition of the novel, and particularly the prologue and its relation to the rest of the story. In the next chapter I shall still be concerned with matters of technique, but I shall be dealing with one specific aspect: the author's manipulation of narrative distance and tone and its attendant effects.

The novel is in three parts, with a prologue and an epilogue, and each part employs a different narrative technique. Part I, which is the longest and most eventful, uses third-person narrative form; Part II uses epistolary form; and Part III uses diary form. D. L. Shaw has suggested that these techniques are "merely elements of variety" and that "it is fruitless to try to justify them" (*11*, p. 22); but Eamonn Rodgers has argued that these changes in technique have as their function to aid the novelist in bringing out the basic theme of the novel: solitude (*10*). Since Rodgers is the only critic to have paid any attention to this important subject, it is appropriate, even mandatory, to consider at this point what he has to say on the subject.

In Part I of the novel, according to Rodgers, Baroja has deliberately avoided omniscient narration and has seen Sacha almost exlusively from the outside, as she would be seen by another person. Rodgers concedes that Baroja does not maintain the stance of an external observer at all times throughout Part I – on rare occasions, forced by the need to provide the reader with important information, he does allow himself to violate the principle of non-omniscience and looks into the minds of the characters. But overall what Baroja is aiming at is:

> establecer entre el lector y Sacha la misma relación superficial que existe entre las personas en la vida real. Los teóricos de la novela suelen decirnos que se aprende mucho más de un perso-

naje de ficción que de un personaje real. Pero esto no puede ser
verdad si se emplea la técnica narrativa que utiliza Baroja
aquí, técnica que imita con una fidelidad asombrosa la imper-
fección de nuestro conocimiento de las personas que pasan a
nuestro lado o incluso de aquellos con quienes intimamos.
(*10*, p. 578)

Baroja's problem, argues Rodgers, stems from the fact that he
is dealing with a difficult subject, "el de comunicar la no
comunicación" (*10*, p. 580). Baroja's use of the epistolary form
in Part II is unconventional: it avoids the intimate revelation of
a character's mind and soul typical of the eighteenth-century
epistolary novel. Instead of allowing for the communication of
the self, it points rather to its isolation. The seemingly inconsequential touristic reportage is there to underline the lack of a
bond between the world of the mind and the material world.
Thus, "Sacha está aislada no sólo de la gente, sino también del
mundo exterior" (*10*, p. 584). The change from epistolary to
diary technique marks a further development in Sacha's isolation: with the marriage of Vera she can no longer use her as a
correspondent; now she has to write exclusively for herself. Her
detachment from her milieu is underlined in Part III by her
cultural irrelation in an alien country. Rodgers ends his analysis
by summarizing what he sees as the fundamental theme of the
novel:

> La visión pesimista de Baroja, en esta novela tan característica
> de él, no es una mera idiosincrasia personal o una postura
> ideológica. Es más bien una conciencia de que la coherencia de
> la sociedad burguesa, y la satisfacción que el burgués experi-
> mentaba de pertenecer de lleno a su ciudad, su país y su época,
> se han esfumado de repente, dejando al individuo completa-
> mente desarraigado y solo. (*10*, p. 589)

The importance of Rodgers's study lies in the way in which it
brings out the thematic coherence of the novel and in which it
relates this to the technique employed by the author. *El mundo
es ansí* is a novel about human isolation, isolation from one's
natural milieu and isolation from one's fellow humans, and
Baroja's arrangement of his story helps to support this theme. It is
difficult to disagree with this sensitive and sympathetic reading

of *El mundo es ansí*, but certain aspects still remain unexplained: the personality of the narrator of the prologue; the need for the epilogue; the difference in tone between Part I on the one hand and Parts II and III on the other; the particular way that Sacha writes; and the curious violations of non-omniscient narration.

The three-chapter prologue is an integral part of the work and plays a crucial role. Its most important function is to establish the basis of the story and the existence of an agent through whom the story is brought to light. In the prologue the reader listens to a narrator who has his own identity and personality. This narrator does not speak much *of* himself but he certainly speaks *as* himself. The first person plural of "los que nos sentimos vagos de profesión" (p. 33) and "todos sabemos" (p. 34) very soon gives way to a quite unambiguous first person singular:

> Varias veces *vi* a Velasco en Madrid y en Sevilla, casi siempre con gente del bronce, y *me* habló de sus proyectos ...
> Un día al final del verano estaba *yo* en un pueblecito de la costa vasca, cuando *recibí* un telegrama. (p. 35. My italics)

For the remainder of the prologue narrator and characters exist on the same level. The narrator attends the wedding of Velasco and Sacha and accompanies them on their excursions in the Basque countryside. Years later, he receives a slightly enigmatic and melancholy letter from Sacha, and later still he meets Velasco, who rather curtly announces that his marriage ended in separation. Finally in the prologue the narrator makes the acquaintance of a Swiss lady who has lived in Russia and who has news of Sacha Savarof:

> La señora aquella conocía la vida de Sacha en todos sus detalles; quería convencerme de lo protervo de la conducta de los hombres en general y de los españoles en particular.
> Probablemente sólo con este objeto, me invitó a ir a su casa y me contó la vida de Sacha, y me dejó para que leyera un paquete de cartas y unos apuntes que había escrito la rusa mientras estaba en España. (p. 44)

This provides the clue to the narrative disposition of the novel. Part I is told by the narrator-agent in third-person form and is based on what he heard from the Swiss lady; Part II reproduces the letters which Sacha wrote to her friend Vera Petrovna and which the Swiss lady lent to the narrator; and Part III reconstructs Sacha's diaries on the basis of her own notes. Three people are therefore involved in telling the story of Sacha Savarof: Sacha herself, the narrator-agent of the prologue and the Swiss lady. But who are these two unnamed people, and what are their roles?

The Swiss lady of the prologue who produces Sacha's letters and notes is Madame Frossard, her tutor in Moscow, later her landlady in Geneva, and finally Vera's landlady in that same city. The identification is not positively made by the narrator in the prologue because the Swiss lady is not named, and the inference is left to be drawn by the reader later on. The inference is not only fully justified but even necessary. A casual reading of the novel may overlook the role of Madame Frossard and fail to connect her with the unnamed Swiss lady of the prologue, since on the six occasions when she is mentioned this is done very briefly (pp. 49, 54–5, 66, 68, 73, 99). But the details provided by Baroja, scant as they are, can leave little doubt that one is dealing here with one person and not two. Like Madame Frossard, the lady of the prologue is Swiss, comes from Geneva, has lived in Russia, and frequents pedagogic circles. Another lady who is also mentioned in the prologue, in Sacha's letter to the narrator ("Pienso volver a mi país, a casa de una antigua amiga de mi pobre madre a la que tengo cariño y que me quiere todavía ...", p. 42), makes an even more fleeting appearance later in the story: "Vivía entonces [Sacha's mother] en la casa de una señora amiga suya ..." (p. 50). Also fascinating is Velasco's passing reference in the prologue to his cousin: "no le hubiera molestado a usted si un imbécil de primo mío hubiera venido aquí como prometió" (p. 35). How ironical that this cousin who absents himself from Velasco's wedding will later be the indirect cause, even the direct cause, of the break-up of his marriage! Baroja throws in these details apparently quite casually without directly telling the reader where the connections lie. The connections are quite deliberate, but they are in no way forced or overdrawn, as if Baroja were reluctant to reveal the artifice or to make things easy for the reader. At any rate these various cross-references show an almost fastidious attention to detail on the part of the novelist.

So much then for the identity of the Swiss lady. What about the identity of the narrator-agent himself? Clearly there is no name we can ascribe to him, for at no time is his name disclosed. But we do learn something of him. Right from the opening lines of the book the narrator points to himself as being an artist of some sort when, talking of Velasco, he uses the first person plural: "El arte es un mullido lecho para los que nos sentimos vagos de profesión" (p. 33). Shortly afterwards he refers to himself as "un desocupado" (p. 37), suggesting that he does not have an occupation that requires regular attendance at a place of work. In the second chapter of the prologue the occupation of the narrator is revealed when he tells us that he sent Sacha one of his books. His profession is confirmed much later, in Sacha's diary, when she refers to him as "ese escritor español a quien he conocido en Biarritz" (p. 128). This Spanish writer is from a town not too far from La Rioja (province of Logroño), he likes to spend his holidays on the Basque coast, and Sacha, when she writes to him, calls the region she visited with him after the wedding "su país" (p. 42). Clearly this Spaniard is a Basque. What little direct description we get of the narrator also comes via Sacha, who labels him *apático*, *meditabundo*, *algo gris*, epithets which bring the public side of Baroja's person to mind. It thus looks as if Baroja, in inventing a narrator-agent and putting him on the same plane as the characters, is in effect finding a footing for himself in the novel, for the association author-narrator is more than hinted at. But why does Baroja need to create a fictional alter-ego and to present him – and therefore by association himself – as the editor, rather than as the inventor, of the story?

At first sight it would seem that Baroja is using the traditional device of the 'editor' in order to provide his story with structural verisimilitude, in other words to give the narration an internal justification for its existence: this editor, having made the acquaintance of the protagonist, later comes across some documents written by her, is struck by those writings, and decides to reconstruct her life and to publish the documents. But further consideration of the question strongly suggests that structural verisimilitude is not the major aim of Baroja in employing this device. The first thing that one misses is the usual declaration from

the editor that the account which follows is based on sources un-
covered and information received: having mentioned what
appear to be his sources, he then fails to add that his role will be
merely that of editor; the usual disclaimer of paternity is missing.
This small but curious omission is a departure from a well-worn
practice that hints at a less than conventional use of fictional devices. Just as conspicuously missing is Madame Frossard's explanation of how Sacha's letters to Vera and Sacha's personal
diaries came to be in her possession, an explanation that would
have presented no problems at all: Vera was living at Madame
Frossard's *pensión* at the time when Sacha was writing to her,
and later on, after the last entry in the diary, Sacha revisits
Switzerland twice and would quite naturally have called on her
old tutor and ladlady. Nor is there any mention of the language
of redaction of the letters and diaries. The language would presumably have been Russian, but the editor of these documents,
unlike the editor of Cide Hamete's chronicle in *Don Quixote*,
does not bother to hire the services of a translator, a simple enough
expedient.[21] All these three points are so obvious that Baroja's
failure to deal with them is not only surprising but even poten-
tially significant, particularly in the light of his meticulous attention to detail in other respects. Baroja knew the novelist's stock-
in-trade perfectly well – as is amply demonstrated by his use
of a variety of similar technical tricks in the historical series
Memorias de un hombre de acción –, and if he did not bring it to
bear on the case of *El mundo es ansí* it may have been because he
was seeking some other effect or following some other line of
thought.

The partial obscurity in which Baroja has preferred to leave the
editorial genesis of Sacha's story is again apparent in the prologue's relationship in time to the rest of the story. Once again it
is not possible to ascribe this to a lack of concern on the part
of the novelist for the finer details of narrative chronology: an
examination of the time-span of the main events of the story
from the time of Sacha's first marriage to the end of her second
reveals a close attention to the time factor. It is worth insisting

[21] In this connection, it is interesting to note that in the prologue Baroja does
make a point of telling us that Sacha's letter to the narrator was in French.

on this because inattentive readers have sometimes accused Baroja of being slipshod. Sacha and Klein decide to get married in spring (p. 87). The wedding probably takes place in mid-spring, because the weather, though fine, is changeable, and the girls, lightly clad, are taken by surprise by a sudden squall (p. 93). The *viaje de bodas* does not take place immediately but a little later, in early June (p. 96). Sacha and Klein live in Geneva for over a year (p. 98). Some eighteen months after her marriage Sacha is recalled to Russia (p. 98); the arrival in that country therefore takes place in the autumn. At the end of a further two years her marriage is at an end (p. 102) and she has to wait seven or eight months for the divorce to come through. Approximately four years have elapsed since her wedding, and we would therefore expect it to be spring when Sacha goes to Florence (p. 103); and indeed in her second letter to Vera she describes the events of Holy Saturday in Florence (p. 107). The following summer is spent in Bellagio (p. 126), and the holiday is concluded in Biarritz. Her marriage to Velasco takes place at the end of September (p. 127), which agrees precisely with what we read in the prologue (p. 35). Sacha's diary is therefore begun in the early autumn, and sure enough we find references to the harvest, to the mists and to the increasing coldness of the weather and bareness of the trees. The village folk attend the All Souls novena, which points to the time of year very precisely: late October, early November. In Madrid the rainy season is well under way; in Andalusia the olives are being picked and the oranges are ripening on the trees. Later there is a passing reference to Christmas, after which Arcelu appears, and on his initiative a stove is installed in Sacha's hotel room. The break between Sacha and Velasco occurs that same winter; when Sacha arrives in Moscow after her flight it is snowing heavily. Sacha spends the spring in Moscow, and with the arrival of summer goes to Geneva to visit her friend Vera. There is therefore no problem in following the chronology of the novel. Sacha's daughter, Olga, provides a good example of the care taken by the novelist to avoid inconsistencies without at the same time giving too many precise details. Olga is only a few months old when her parents leave for Russia (p. 99). She then lives in Russia with them for about two years, and then another

seven or eight months in the company of her mother after her
father's departure. At the time of her arrival in Florence she must
have been about three years old, and therefore when her mother
married for the second time she had to be about three and a half.
And this is her age as the narrator of the prologue estimates it:
"una niña de tres o cuatro años" (p. 37). Even in such a relatively
small matter Baroja has been careful enough to ensure that he did
not get his sums wrong.

Reverting now to the prologue, it is obvious that the marriage
between Sacha and Velasco at which the narrator acts as witness
fits chronologically between Part II and Part III of the novel. But
precisely when did Sacha write her letter to the narrator? Rodolfo
Cardona, in his essay on *El mundo es ansí*, says that Sacha's letter
"corresponde, en el esquema temporal de la novela, al final del
capítulo XX, penúltimo de la tercera parte" (*3*, p. 570). This is
incorrect, and there are two reasons for believing this to be so.
Firstly, at the end of chapter XX of Part III Sacha goes to Moscow
via Paris, Berlin and Warsaw, and there is no mention whatever
of her having stayed in Switzerland, from where the narrator
received the letter. Secondly, the narrator mentions that between
his meeting Sacha and his receiving news from her "transcu-
rrieron varios años" (p. 41), and Sacha's second marriage, the
period covered by chapters I to XX of Part III, lasts no more
than six months, so the letter could not possibly have been written
just after Sacha had left Spain. All one can say is that Sacha wrote
the letter some very considerable time after her separation from
Velasco and her departure from Spain. It was not even written at
the time of the events in the epilogue, during Sacha's visit to her
friend Vera in Geneva, because, although the letter is written
in Switzerland, Sacha mentions in it that she is staying "a orillas
del lago Leman, en un pueblo, en una casa antigua, inmensa,
fría y triste" (p. 42), which does not sound at all like the house
of her friend described in the epilogue. The possibility of making
cross-references and providing the story with the appearance of a
self-supporting structure has been disregarded. Baroja has chosen
not to tell us what has happened to Sacha between the epilogue
and her letter to the narrator, nor how much time has elapsed: all
that we can deduce is that Sacha's letter to the narrator is the

latest information that she provides about herself, and the events in the three parts of the novel and in the epilogue antedate the letter in the prologue. The end of the story is thus kept deliberately vague, open-ended, and Sacha's ultimate destiny is unknown. The epilogue informs us of her sense of total loss when she learns that Arcelu has gone to China. Her letter in the prologue underlines her spiritual suffering and melancholia, and her despondency at the prospect of having to return to Russia for good. The narrator's encounter with Madame Frossard merely confirms Sacha's situation in the starkest possible way:

> – ¿Y Sacha? ¿Dónde está?
> – Ahora, en Moscú. Muy mal, la pobre. (p. 44)

Thus Sacha disappears from view as if into an enveloping mist, and neither reader nor narrator will ever know what ultimately becomes of her. Nevertheless the open-endedness of the novel is something that applies only to the plot or story-line. From the point of view of character development Baroja has brought his story to a perfect conclusion, and he has done it in a most unobtrusive way. For in the prologue he has provided us with two tiny but curious details which invite us to draw a most interesting inference. One detail is that Sacha is now separated from her daughter; the other is that she is living in Moscow in the house and in the company of her mother's old friend. Sacha therefore ends up exactly as her mother, leading the life of a refined recluse.[22] And this ending is after all absolutely logical, when we consider, firstly, that when as a child she had visited her mother, Sacha "se impregnó de sus gustos y de sus ideas" (p. 50), and secondly, that she has allowed herself to become increasingly cut off from external reality and has given herself to her own private world of artistic and literary pursuits. Baroja's use of tiny and seemingly inconsequential details that later turn out to be preg-

---

[22] The parallel is quite striking, for apart from the two points I have mentioned, several of the things the narrator says about Sacha's mother (pp. 49–50) are equally applicable to Sacha: an impressionable woman, unable to live with an impulsive husband, in a poor state of health, steeped in melancholia and with no hope for the future, and even *extranjerizada* (Sacha admits to a similar feeling about Russia).

nant with significance is one of the most demanding aspects of his art.

Eamonn Rodgers has put forward the view that the invention of an editor in *El mundo es ansí* is due to Baroja's wish to avoid omniscient narration: "[Baroja] parece haber encontrado artificial la convención de la narración omnisciente" (*10*, p. 578). I am inclined to agree with this, but the trouble is that Baroja appears to have found just about every technique of novel writing artificial. The most frequent narrative point of view in his novels, at least in those of the first period, is one of restricted omniscience, that is to say one in which an impersonal narrator allows himself to look into the mind of the central character but sees all other characters only from the outside. Is the narrator of *El mundo es ansí* omniscient or non-omniscient? Is his knowledge limited to what he observes, to what he reads, to what he hears other people say? One should not see this in black and white terms, since in practice complete omniscience and complete non-omniscience are rare. But one can ask just how far Baroja has gone towards eliminating omniscient narration.

The Spanish writer of the prologue functions also as a narrator within the body of the novel. Part I of the novel is based on what the Swiss lady, Madame Frossard, tells him, but Madame Frossard is not the narrator. It is important here to avoid making a false assumption, namely that the narrator of Part I is the Swiss lady of the prologue. In his essay, Rodolfo Cardona argues that despite the "disimulo" of employing a "narradora" in Part I, it is easy to detect the voice of the author: "Hasta [en] la primera parte, narrada en tercera persona y, por consiguiente, la más impersonal de todas las secciones de la novela, encontramos descripciones con una adjetivación subjetiva imposible de atribuir a la narradora a quien el autor nos había presentado en el prólogo como una feminista" (*3*, p. 568). But the consequence – in my opinion unavoidable – of this misinterpretation is to turn Baroja into a hack novelist who forgets who his narrator is and puts incongruous words in her mouth. If one sees the narrator of Part I as the Swiss lady one is also left in the awkward situation of having to explain why, when she appears in her own narration, she should refer to herself in the third person. These difficulties, however, do not arise if we accept that the narrator of Part I is, not the Swiss lady of the prologue, but the Spanish writer of the prologue. The account of the Swiss lady is not given verbatim by the narrator: this much is apparent if one compares the narrator's account with his description, at the end of the prologue, of the lady's own account. What the narrator has done is to use Madame Frossard's account, but he himself is not just a neutral instrument of communication. Indeed, the whole work, from beginning to end, must be seen as the work of this editor-narrator, and even the letters and particularly the diary could be assumed to have gone through some sort of editorial process, as I shall shortly mention.

Having established, then, that the editor of Sacha's writings is also the narrator of Part I, one can now proceed to ask whether he functions as an omniscient or as a non-omniscient narrator. Baroja begins by making the narrator a character in his own story, and this has the immediate effect of making the reader expect a non-omniscient narration. But in fact this apparent attempt at limiting the narrator's point of view and making it congruent with what would obtain outside the realm of a novel is not sustained. At certain moments the narrator ceases to write as a character with a restricted vision and proceeds to acquire authorial omniscience. Eamonn Rodgers has pointed out some instances of this and has argued that they are an exigency of the plot: the reader needs to see some characters from inside, even if only slightly. This one may accept, though with reservations.[23] One could also pass over as normal novelistic licence both the passages of conversation at which Madame Frossard was not present and the detailed knowledge of characters which the narrator shows in Part I, a knowledge which, realistically, could not have come to him via Madame Frossard because the latter would scarcely have been in a position to have it: but this sort of absolute realism is rare in imaginative literature. There is, however, a great deal more in Part I which must be classed as

---

[23] With reservations because passages in which the narrator looks into the mind of Sacha are by no means as rare as Rodgers seems to believe; see for instance pp. 57, 68, 75, 87, 96, for passages in which Sacha's mental processes are described.

omniscient narration. Here are just a few of many possible examples:

> La señorita del mostrador, una muchacha muy bonita, distinguía a Klein con su amistad; él, al entrar, la saludaba y le daba la mano, pero no quería galantearla ... (p. 71)

> Semenevski rio silenciosamente de la repuganacia de Vera. (p. 83)

> Vera miró a Semenevski sospechando si en sus palabras habría algo de ironía. (p. 85)

> Semenevski le dijo a Afsaguin confidencialmente que había datos para sospechar que la Staël tenía tendencias sóficas ... (p. 91)

> Cuando dejaron a los recién casados, volvieron Semenevski y su mujer, Afsaguin y Vera hacia Carouge.
> Había cesado de llover. La noche estaba estrellada, magnífica.
> De pronto Afsaguin se detuvo y murmuró:
> – Semenevski. ¡Eh!
> – ¿Qué pasa?
> – Napoleón a Fouché ... *Par la gendarmerie.* – y Afsaguin tuvo que pararse retorciéndose de risa. (p. 94)

These extracts are all clear examples of omniscient narration, they relate things that could not possibly be known by a non-omniscient narrator; yet they could not be said to be essential from the point of view of the development of the story: if Baroja had wanted to avoid omniscient narration he could quite easily have left them out. At the end of Part II, the narrator resumes the narration after transcribing Sacha's letters to Vera:

> Al acercarse el verano, al llegar los primeros calores, Sacha decidió ir a veranear a Bellagio, un pueblecito ideal que está entre los dos brazos del lago de Como. (p. 126)

Again this is presented as coming from an omniscient narrator, since the information is not in Sacha's diary nor does Madame Frossard figure in her life at this point. Yet Baroja could very easily have inserted a comment to the effect that the narrator received the information from Sacha herself at the time of her wedding to Velasco which took place later that summer. Indeed the technique of having one character (usually a secondary one) tell another character (usually the protagonist) of something that happens off-stage is a very common one in early Baroja, and is used with the object of keeping the attention focussed on the main character and not diffusing it over the whole range of characters. It is in effect a way of restricting, though not eliminating, the omniscience of the narrator.[24] But in *El mundo es ansí* Baroja does not use all the possibilities of this technique. When the narrator once again takes over the narration in the epilogue, he demonstrates a knowledge that is not in keeping with the limited range and vision he shows in the prologue. One could perhaps make the assumption that Madame Frossard had learnt that Sacha had written to Arcelu's sister, since Sacha was in Geneva at the time, though one would need to assume too that she discovered that "Margarita le contestó a vuelta de correo" and that "al leer esta carta Sacha se encerró en su cuarto y estuvo llorando" (p. 184). Indeed none of this is impossible, and it would no doubt have been very convenient and satisfying for the critic and the reader who like a neatly-packaged product if Baroja had included a statement to the effect that Sacha, after visiting her friend Vera, went to stay at the *pensión* Frossard; but the statement is conspicuous for its absence. And the work of course ends on a fully omniscient note: "Y el lema del escudo de Navaridas le vino otra vez a la imaginación" (p. 184). The epilogue is thus presented as coming from an omniscient narrator, and, what is more significant, it is there despite the fact that from the point of view of the plot there was really no need for it. As far as the events themselves are concerned, everything in the epilogue is seen from the point of view of Sacha, and the information could have been included just as easily as part of a continuing diary. But Baroja has chosen to emphasize at the end the pre-eminence of the omniscient narrator.

The foregoing analysis offers sufficient grounds, I believe, for stating that the invention of the whole prologue, with the narrator meeting various characters including the protagonist herself, was

[24] This technique has been well studied by Hugh Probyn (*9*, pp. 93–103).

not due to a desire on the part of the author either for structural verisimilitude or for non-omniscient narration. Why, then, employ this artifice? Is it just Baroja's idiosyncratic way of fictionalizing a real-life experience? For it is well known that in 1909 Baroja was best man at his friend Paul Schmitz's wedding to a Russian woman in the Orthodox chapel in Biarritz, and the description of the wedding appears in the first chapter of the prologue.[25] But he could just as easily have included the description in a third-person narration or in Sacha's diary and have thus avoided the invention of the narrator of the prologue. Also, while his experience at Schmitz's wedding may have given Baroja the initial idea for a novel, it is quite simply inconceivable that the prologue as it stands was written before the body of the novel. There are so many minute but accurate references – one almost every few lines – to events, people and places that occur in the body of the work, that the prologue must have been either written or at the very least carefully revised after Parts I, II and III were finished.

The artifice of the prologue does serve of course to introduce an editor, and Sacha's writings need an editor if they are to be brought to light. Madame Frossard herself could have been used in this role: she had Sacha's writings in her possession and she had the necessary knowledge of her earlier life and background. But Baroja chose to invent a third figure to intervene in the editorial process. Eamonn Rodgers has said that Baroja, in order to give an impression of objectivity and to avoid omniscient narration, converts the narrator into a mere transcriber (*10*, p. 578). Is this really so? Has the editor-narrator limited himself to transcribing Sacha's writings? It is an interesting point, and while there is no way of telling for certain whether the diary has been transcribed faithfully and in its entirety, Baroja tantalizingly raises the possibility of the diary having been in some way tampered with by the editor. When Sacha mentions, apparently for the first time, her acquaintance with the Spanish writer, she

[25] Velasco is not, however, based on Paul Schmitz, despite the view of Cardona (*3*, p. 546). Baroja was fond of Schmitz, and Velasco is depicted unsympathetically. And anyway the editor-narrator refers to Velasco as "conocido nada más" (p. 44).

calls him "ese escritor español" (p. 128) rather than "un escritor español". Then there are no dates in the diary, which is unusual. Each new entry in the diary is not separately marked, the division into chapters seldom corresponding to separate entries: some chapters represent several different moments of redaction and include separate entries. And the role of an active editor is clearly implied in a few of the chapter headings. None of these points is in itself very significant; but in all they are typical of the strange way in which many things in this novel are constantly suggested yet never fully explained, which brings us back to the question of the role of the editor-narrator.

5 *Narrative distance in* El mundo es ansí

The editor-narrator of *El mundo es ansí* is a writer who shares several characteristics with Pío Baroja the author; there is in fact no very real distinction we can make between the two, and the editor-narrator can be regarded as the author's professional mask. The device is by no means confined to *El mundo es ansí*, for Baroja found a little niche for himself – or rather for an authorial persona – in the prologues and introductory chapters of several novels: *Camino de perfección, El mayorazgo de Labraz, César o nada, El laberinto de las sirenas, Los pilotos de altura, Las noches del Buen Retiro, Locuras de carnaval*, and the three novels in *Agonías de nuestro tiempo*. No research appears to have been done in this area of Barojan technique, but the object of the device would seem to be to raise in the mind of the reader the question of the relation in which the author or narrator stands to his story and to the protagonist. This, I would argue, is true of *El mundo es ansí*.

If the editor-narrator does not quite ascribe to himself the authorship or invention of the story he is narrating, he does at any rate function with almost the same freedom that he enjoys in his alleged profession, the freedom of an author inventing his story and his characters. The narrator's attitudes are really the author's attitudes, or, perhaps more accurately, the attitudes the author wants us to ascribe to him. The whole prologue bears a distinct personal stamp, and even if the narrator does not bother to tell us much about himself he leaves us in no doubt that he has his own personality and ideas. The ironic tone of the prologue is evident in various little touches that clearly reveal the voice of the narrator:

> Todos sabemos, por haberlo leído en los folletines franceses, que los viajes y los clásicos sirven para formar la juventud y completar la educatión. (p. 34)

> Se me figuraba ver un romano de los antiguos tiempos con alguna joven escita robada en las selvas vírgenes de la ignorada Europa. (p. 36)

El mozo del hotel tenía un aire tan extraño y tan solemne, con los pelos negros encrespados, la nariz corva, dirigida amenazadoramente hacia el cielo, la actitud gallarda y los guantes blancos en las manos cruzadas, que me daba ganas de reír.

Para dominar la inoportuna tendencia a la risa, me puse lo más compungido posible, haciéndome cuenta de que me encontraba en una ceremonia fúnebre. (p. 38)

The narrator's attitude is even more clearly discernible in the way he depicts Velasco, of whom he gives a pointedly sardonic view:

Pronto Velasco pudo dar un juicio de técnico consumado acerca de Botticelli, de Donatello, del champagne de la viuda Clicquot, de la bailarinas de music-halls más ilustres ... (p. 34)

En arte Velasco no aceptaba más que lo genuinamente español, lo castellano castizo, y cuanto más crudo y más violento le parecía mejor. (p. 34)

– Créalo usted, no se puede vivir con una mujer sin religión.
Yo le contemplé con un poco de asombro.
– Ya ha llegado usted a considerar la religión como cosa útil, ¿eh? – le dije.
–Sí, me parece útil para los demás – contestó él categóricamente.
Y hablamos de otra cosa. (p. 43)

Velasco may feel that his acquaintance with the narrator is sufficiently well established to offer him hospitality for a full week, but the narrator has no illusions about the nature of the relationship: his contempt for Velasco is thinly veiled.

Thus, although in the prologue the narrator does not on the whole express his opinions directly, his personality nevertheless comes through strongly in the ironic tone and comments. He looks down with either contempt or amusement at what is going on. The marriage ceremony strikes him as risible, Velasco as contemptible and Sacha as delightfully naive. His is an attitude of complete detachment and superiority which only momentarily gives way to human concern when he receives the slightly pathetic letter from Sacha, a letter which, he confesses, "me produjo impresión" (p. 43). That the ironic tone of the prologue is due to the personality of the editor-narrator is confirmed by the persistence of this tone in Part I, in which he is still in charge of the narration. Ironic touches like those in the prologue still occur in Part I. Here are some examples:

> Hay algunos fisiólogos que suponen que mientras la sutura frontal del cráneo no se cierra definitivamente, el cerebro puede seguir desarrollándose y creciendo. Sin duda a Savarof esta sutura se le cerró pronto, cosa bastante frecuente entre los generales rusos y de los demás países. (p. 45)

> La característica del profesor Ornsom era la sociología lírica ... (p. 62)

> Unos escalones solamente separaban el escenario donde se cantaban los efectos digestivos del rancho del escenario donde se explicaban los efectos de la Revolución social. (p. 82)

> En este momento de furor del conferenciante, en el que aparecía como un energúmeno, las luces eléctricas oscilaron como asustadas y concluyeron por apagarse.
> — Esos canallas de burgueses — dijo uno — quieren sumirnos en la oscuridad.
> — Luz, luz — gritaron varios.
> — Luz y Revolución Social — exclamó la voz de Afsaguin. (p. 84)

The irony of the last comment belongs fully and exclusively to the narrator. Afsaguin, as the narrative makes clear, is at this moment too enthralled and fired with ideological enthusiasm to realize the comic effect of his words.

In addition to ironic remarks such as the preceding ones, we also find in Part I certain sententious comments or reflections. Here are just two examples:

> Hay en el amor, como en todo lo que se expresa con labios humanos, una retórica hábil y artificiosa que da apariencias de vida a lo que está muerto y aspectos de brillantez a lo que es opaco. Es una mentira que a la luz de la ilusión tiene el carácter de la verdad; es una mentira que se defiende con cariño. (p. 87)

> La literatura ha hecho creer a los hombres y a las mujeres que en determinadas circunstancias se desarrollan en ellos fuerzas espirituales que les llevan a las alturas en una felicidad inefable. La palabrería literaria ha dado aire a esta idea, y para justificarla se ha inventado la psicología femenina. Efectivamente; nada

mejor para explicar una cosa problemática que inventar otra tan
problemática y darla como indiscutible. (p. 94)

Many other similar comments could be adduced. Chapter XVII of
Part I is particularly rich in personal generalizations on the part of
the narrator; and chapter VIII offers comments on the Genevan
aristocracy which reveal the same strongly subjective bias.

This bias is detectable also in the distance between narrator and
fictional protagonist. This is not to say that the depiction of Sacha
is ironic; it is not. But neither is it totally sympathetic, as my
analysis in chapter III has already suggested. The detached tone of
the narrator persists even when he looks at Sacha, which of course
he does a great deal of the time. And by this I do not mean that
Sacha is looked at only from outside; she is looked at both from
outside and from inside. What I mean is that the narrator's norms
are by and large not Sacha's norms. Here are some illustrations of
this.

It is clear that the narrator does not approve of the refined aesthetic seclusion of Sacha's mother: "La madre de Sacha era una
mujer excesivamente impresionable, desequilibrada, neurasténica
... Vivía ... recluída, como una flor de estufa, leyendo los libros
de Turgueneff y tocando en el piano a Beethoven" (p. 49). Sacha
on the other hand, though at this stage she is still far from adopting such a posture herself, "admiraba a su madre como criatura
refinada, espiritual y artista" (p. 50). An even clearer dissociation
between the narrator and Sacha occurs over the question of
Savarof's confinement of his daughter during the revolutionary
troubles of 1905: whereas the narrator judges Savarof to be on
this occasion "prudente y cauto", for Sacha the actions of her father
are "egoístas y mezquinas" (p. 54). Similarly over Professor Ornsom: whilst the narrator leaves the reader in absolutely no doubt
as to what he thinks of Ornsom, whom he calls "cuco y farsante"
(p. 62), Sacha falls prey to the ideological oratory of the professor.
Another, and major, divergence between the narrator and Sacha
is furnished by Klein. The narrator's view of Klein is unsym-
pathetic right from the start, and becomes increasingly hostile as
Sacha finds him increasingly likeable. Indeed Sacha herself is
criticized by the narrator for allowing herself to be duped by
Klein's superficial charm and failing to see into his real motives:

"¡Es tan fácil seguir al que promete la felicidad sin esfuerzo!"
(p. 74). Sacha's lack of insight into human character is not the only
thing criticized by the narrator. Sacha's error lies not only in her
choice of partner but also in the way she falls in love: "Sacha se
dejaba llevar por el encanto de la Naturaleza y por el encanto de
las palabras" (p. 87), but this, for the narrator, is "una retórica
hábil y artificiosa", "una mentira", a dangerous illusion engendered
by sentimental literature. Just as earlier the narrator had pointed to
Sacha's impracticality and naivety in the way she addressed herself to the downtrodden Russian peasants, now he points to her
lack of awareness in the way she forms a romantic attachment.
The narrator of course shows no signs of hostility, contempt or dislike towards Sacha as he does towards certain other characters; but
he does show some signs of disapproval, and it is clear that in
several important respects he does not share her attitudes.

The ironic remarks, the sententious comments, the implied, even
at times explicit, criticism of the protagonist: all three aspects reveal the voice, loud and clear, of the narrator in Part I, a narrator
who does not limit himself to narrating but who offers his opinions
and comments on people and events. In Part II there is a change of
narrator – now what we read are the letters of Sacha to Vera
Petrovna – and this change is accompanied by a change in tone.
The irony which is present in Part I and in the prologue disappears, and instead of the detached and superior tone we find a certain sympathy and warmth tinged with sadness and sentimentality.
The transition from an ironic to a sentimental tone is very noticeable, and, apart from the obvious fact that the change was intended
to coincide with the change in narrator, must have involved the
novelist in a conscious effort to alter the point of view in the story.
The note of sentimentality that is struck in Part II is not loud; it
is nevertheless noticeable in several things: in Sacha's intermittent
references to her own situation which convey a sense of loneliness;
in the feeling of pity that Sacha expresses for some other characters;
in the concern she shows for the happy outcome of the Petrovna-
Leskoff affair; and not least of all in some of the descriptions which
add to the atmosphere of gentle melancholy. By contrast, the editor-
narrator's intromission at the end of Part II is curt, detached, un-
emotional, and even reveals once again his amused disdain for cer-

tain characters: "Velasco tenía la humorada de encontrar empalagosos y sin interés los paisajes del lago de Como y decirlo a todas horas" (p. 127).

The delicate confessional tone is re-established as soon as Sacha takes over the narration in Part III. The diary technique, coupled with Sacha's brief but frequent references to her own situation and above all with the manner of her writing, makes the reader feel closer than ever to her, and the narrative acquires a greater degree of intimacy. The distancing effect noticeable in Part I between narrator and protagonist, and therefore between reader and protagonist, disappears as we listen directly to Sacha herself. So successful is the technique that we soon begin to identify with Sacha and unconsciously to share her judgments. When, at the end of Sacha's narration, the editor-narrator returns with the epilogue, his objective detachment, though still present, has lost its earlier effect. He it is who points to Sacha's half-hearted attempt to re-establish her relationship with Vera; and he it is who points to her self-interest in writing to Arcelu's sister apologizing for her abrupt departure. But it is done without any expressed criticism, as if the narrator too, like the reader, had moved closer to Sacha and to an appreciation of her predicament. Even in its more muted and unobtrusive form, his voice is still significant. The final view of Sacha, the view that the reader is invited to retain, is the view of the narrator, and it is a particular view. But before finally considering the closing lines of the book, it is necessary to study in detail Baroja's technique in those parts of the book in which the narrative voice is that of Sacha herself.

I have just said that as a result of the diary technique the reader feels closer to Sacha and unconsciously begins to identify with her outlook and to share her judgments. It is easy to assume that the epistolary and diary techniques are trustworthy, in other words that they offer the reader access to the genuine inner life of the character. But this can be a false assumption. Writing letters and diaries can be a way of fabricating a self rather than of revealing it. They may also, it is true, be perfectly sincere and unaffected; but if so this will not be a quality of the epistolary or diary technique, it will be a quality of the writer. All writing about oneself involves a degree of exhibitionism, particularly of course where

the writing is intended for others' attention. Sacha herself makes a
similar observation:

> Hay en todos los hombres y mujeres un fondo de comediante,
> que exige un espectador, e impulsa muchas veces a los mayores
> absurdos por sostener el papel. No es raro que una misma per-
> sona sea el espectador y el cómico al mismo tiempo. (p. 117)[26]

It would perhaps be too far-fetched to see an intended double
meaning in the word *papel*, but the fact remains that Sacha is writing, and is writing about her own situation, about herself, even if
she does, on the whole, avoid cloying self-pity. Is Sacha becoming
a spectator of herself, creating an image of herself? Is she, in her
determination to avoid the worst kind of self-indulgent sentimentality, going to the other extreme of affecting self-objectification? For one is as much a pose as the other, indeed the second
even more so than the first. Apart from what they tell us about her
life, how do Sacha's writings serve to characterize her?

There is undoubtedly a degree of self-objectification in Parts II
and III of *El mundo es ansí*. In Part II Sacha is aware of an observer,
a reader in the person of Vera Petrovna, but, as I said a moment
ago, she is also aware of the danger of playing a role, and she mentions this to her friend (in the quotation given above), and then
refers to herself as an example of her ideas:

> Esto, en parte, es consecuencia de la sugestión que nos produce
> la idea que tienen de nosotros los demás. Mis amigos creen que
> soy generosa, pues efectivamente delante de ellos lo soy. ¿Creen
> que soy buena o mala, pérfida o coqueta? Pues su opinión obra
> en mí, aunque no lo quiera; me da reforzado, amplificado, un
> aspecto de mi manera de ser. Luego yo tomo la opinión, la
> opinión ajena, e intento adaptarme a ella. (p. 118)

The phrase *sostener el papel* occurs for the second time immediately
after this: ". . . no intentes sostener tu papel ni aun delante de mí
misma" (p. 118). Does this suggest, conversely, that it is really
Sacha who is sustaining a role in front of her friend? There is
perhaps some element of jealousy in the interest she shows in Leskoff, but this is not unnatural in view of the fact that Leskoff had

[26] We are here very close to Shanti Andía's "desdoblamiento de mi persona en
narrador y lector".

earlier been in love with her. We may also wonder about Sacha's motives in wishing to join her friend – a wish she twice expresses – during Leskoff's courtship of Vera, a project which would at best have been undiplomatic, given Leskoff's earlier inclination. Nevertheless the only evidence that Sacha is not being entirely truthful with her friend is that provided by the editor-narrator to the effect that she hides from Vera her growing dependence upon Velasco: "Sacha no contó en sus cartas a Vera el final de su estancia en Florencia; no se atrevía a decirle cómo Velasco iba interviniendo en su vida y captándose su voluntad" (p. 126). The reason for her reluctance to confide in Vera is her fear of appearing naive and immature. She does not want to admit the doubts about her feelings for Velasco after offering a great deal of advice in her capacity as a woman of experience: "Mi pequeña Vera, yo tengo, por mi matrimonio poco afortunado, alguna más experiencia que tú, y creo que te puedo aconsejar" (p. 116). This reluctance to be completely truthful with her friend, and by extension perhaps with herself, can be construed as self-objectification. Sacha has given the impression that she is experienced, worldly-wise, a sad but stoically resigned woman who has learnt life's lesson the hard way. She does not tell the whole truth, however, and the narrator has to intervene directly to put us fully in the picture. This intervention is an important corrective, and has the effect of moving us away from Sacha and making us see her in a more objective light. But we are not dealing here with a case of blatant insincerity, we are dealing rather with a woman who in matters concerning the affairs of her own heart suffers from total uncertainty, from an inability to assess her own feelings and those of others correctly until it is too late.

In Part III the question of the reliability of the self-portrait does not really arise. Sacha is not trying to mislead anybody since she is writing only for herself. It would be unwarranted to suppose that Sacha composed her diary with an eye on the reader. True, the diary ultimately gets read and published; but there is nothing which might induce one to think that she had deliberately given it to Madame Frossard with instructions that it should be made to find its way into the hands of the Spanish writer whom she had met in Biarritz. We must accept that the diary is written by Sacha as a purely personal record for her own later reading, and more especially as a way of analyzing her own confused feelings. This, however, in no way means that it has to be taken as an objective record of facts. As I pointed out in chapter III, many of the comments in the diary, far from being objective, are so closely linked to Sacha's own situation that they are meaningful only when related to her personality.

Sacha, then, writes neither to exhibit herself in public nor to project a false image. In this respect we have to accept her account as a sincere, but restrained, expression of her true self: "Prefiero escribir estas páginas para mí sola, conteniéndome un poco para no avergonzarme mañana de mis sentimientos, porque mi experiencia anterior me ha hecho desconfiar un tanto de mi espontaneidad" (p. 128). As part of her emotional and sentimental restraint Sacha will concentrate on writing about her impressions of the world outside. But the very fact that she writes is itself a characterizing element. She has one very important thing in common with her creator and with her editor: the compulsion to turn life into words. She projects her thoughts, her actions, and indeed even her feelings, onto paper. This need to express herself is the most profound trait of her character. *El mundo es ansí* is the story of Sacha's life; but the story of her life is in substantial measure the story of her writings. She herself acknowledges a compulsion to express herself on paper in an attempt to put some order into her own uncertainties and emotional instability. Her writing is part of her effort to get to the bottom of her own self, and as such it characterizes her more than anything else she ever does. Her struggle is a struggle with her own self – with her sentimental weakness which she tries to control, with her inability to analyse correctly her feelings towards other people, with her own sense of rootlessness and personal disorientation. Her writing is an intimate part of herself, part of her own psychology, and there is no way in which we could preserve the figure of Sacha while doing away with her writings. There are therefore good reasons for switching over to first-person narration in Parts II and III of the novel and allowing Sacha to tell her own story. The psychological portrait of Sacha acquires poignancy and depth by virtue of being a self-portrait. What Sacha puts down in writing characterizes her over and above the events she describes. The fact that she puts it down, and the way she puts it down, add another dimension to her characterization; the effect would be lost in a third-person narration. For in Sacha's narration, the record of events – events which could have been recorded equally well in third-person narrative form – is not the significant thing. What is significant about Sacha's letters and diaries is the insight they afford into her personality and predicament. Let us see, then, how Sacha writes, looking first at Part II of the novel.

We get a hint in Part I of what is to come when the narrator indicates Sacha's susceptibility to literature and her sensitivity to the landscape. Her incipient aestheticism will tend increasingly to become a substitute for her unsatisfactory human relationships. This is immediately apparent in the very first letter she writes to Vera. She deliberately shuns company: "El deseo de pasear sola me impulsa a alejarme de la ciudad" (p. 104); when a guide offers to show her around "le digo a todo que no y me meto por un camino entre árboles ..." (p. 106). She goes in search of nature, in search of the "impresiones retinianas" which she says are all she can speak of. But her descriptions are not the concrete and physical ones of an objective tourist guide; their apparent simplicity hides a good deal of subjective vision and stylized rendering:

> ... los árboles brillan con un verde húmedo y obscuro; sobre ellos se destacan con un color delicado los grupos de adelfas en flor. (p. 104)

> Esta fila de cipreses, que avanza trepando por el montecillo, hace un efecto de procesión formada por frailes sombríos y tristes. (p. 105)

> ¡Qué camino más silencioso! ¡Qué admirable! Es un encanto. (p. 106)

> ... los almendros y las adelfas se muestran plagados de flores, y los pájaros cantan entre el follaje húmedo y la lluvia sigue cayendo suavemente. (p. 106)

The contrived delicacy of tone of Sacha's first letter must have struck Vera and she must have mentioned it in her reply, for it prompts Sacha to comment in her second letter, "¿Qué quieres, mi querida Vera? Vive una ya sin esperanza, y para simular la energía que no se tiene, para hacernos la ilusión de abarcar un radio de acción que no abarcamos, están el arte y la música y los libros que son un poco de opio en nuestra vida sin vida" (p. 107). Vera mentions this point again in her next letter, eliciting a similar comment from Sacha: "Notas en mí inclinaciones artísticas. ¿Qué quieres que haga para no aburrirme?" (p. 109). Obliqueness is one of Baroja's most characteristic manners (9, pp. 93–103), and here it is used to convey an outside impression of Sacha even within a larger technique in which everything is seen through Sacha's eyes. Sacha expresses her dislike of any public show of aestheticism, such as that of the young Florentines who put on ecstatic airs at the opera or of her friend María Karolyi who enthuses about Italian painting and sculpture; but she herself cultivates her own private art in the way she translates her life onto paper: phrases like "aspecto melancólico", "ambiente de tristeza" and "soledad completa" occur with relative frequency in the descriptive parts and give the narrative a slightly artificial and certainly a very personal flavour in their evocation of mood. Then there are passages of philosophical reflection (especially in chapters V and VI), and brief but poignant references to her own emotional difficulties: "tengo ganas de llorar", "no hago más que vivir con mis recuerdos", "mi pensamiento está vagando entre Ginebra y Rusia", "salgo ... sin plan, sin rumbo determinado", "he andado hoy a la ventura ..." Even when she refers to other people she is unconsciously projecting her own feelings: "Creo que esos ingleses que vienen después de trabajar mucho a las ciudades célebres por su arte, pensando hallar en éstas un alivio a su tristeza, si se aburren no es porque no tienen sensibilidad, sino porque no encuentran lo que esperaban" (p. 114). Sacha, too, fails to find in Florence "un alivio a su tristeza", and a note of bitterness creeps into her letters as she turns her attention to the Italian way of life only to find it, in her own words, shallow, sordid and repugnant. As her discomfiture increases so do her censures of her friend María Karolyi, an "italianista entusiasta", whom she brands as an aesthete on no fewer than four separate occasions. Her final comment on her friend's gullibility is a slightly cruel one: having listed the various traits and habits of Amati which mark him out to be a lady-killer

and a whoremonger, she adds: "Estos son los hombres que entu-
siasman a las mujeres artistas" (p. 126). Ironically Sacha herself is
all this time falling prey to an artist of a different sort. Her attack
on María's gullibility hides her own uncertainty about Velasco.

All these aspects tend to underline the essentially subjective
nature of Sacha's letter-writing. In addition, Baroja has made use
of an interesting technique of redaction which serves to bring out
the process of Sacha's transformation of reality. The technique consists basically in breaking the logical time-sequence in the narration of an event. The way in which some events are told makes
them chronological impossibilities because Sacha, instead of record-
ing them as they happened in time, records them as she re-lives
them at the moment of writing. The manner of presentation focus-
ses the attention on the writing of the experience rather than on the
experience itself. Here are some examples of this technique.

In chapter III of Part II Sacha relates to Vera her experiences at
the opera the previous night. Sacha begins by casting her mind
back to a past experience, but by the end of the letter that experience has been transferred to the present: "Al terminar la función
hemos marchado de prisa a casa. Ahora, desde mi cuarto, oigo el
ruido de los coches y las conversaciones de la gente que sale del
teatro" (p. 111). The "ayer" of the beginning of the narration is
changed into the "ahora" of the end as Sacha resuscitates the past
experience. The present tense emphasizes the literary nature of the
reconstruction: the experience is really that of creation. In chapter
IX we have another instance of this technique. When Sacha starts
telling her friend of the Amati-Karolyi affair at the beginning of
the letter, the outcome has already taken place: "Aquí ha habido
una pequeña catástrofe en nuestro mundo. El *signor* Amati ha
resultado, como yo creía, un aventurero" (p. 123). But then, as she
considers her friend's anxiety at the first signs of possible disaster,
she switches over to the present:

> El procedimiento sin duda no agrada a María; debe tener miedo
> de averiguar que lo que le dicen es verdad. Sin duda está pren-
> dada del violinista . . .
>   La pobre María no canta ya *l'amour est enfant de Bohème*, y
> creo que se va a convencer de que afortunadamente para ella no
> tiene nada de común con la Tarnowska.

María ha decidido que su padre se entere por la policía de qué clase de hombre es Amati. (p. 124)

In fact Sacha is writing this the day after María's father had received the police report. Indeed there is no problem for the reader in knowing when the events narrated in the letter have taken place: they occurred "hace unos días", "anteayer" and "ayer", so we are not dealing here with a case of authorial confusion. The use of the present tense at certain points allows us more clearly to follow Sacha's own thought processes at the time of writing. The way Sacha keeps slipping into the present tense throughout her nine letters to Vera strongly suggests that what counts is not what happened but the very timelessness of what happened. Many of the actions, although described after they have happened, are described as if they were happening at the moment of writing: "me meto por un camino", "sigo avanzando", "me alejo", "me encuentro perdida". Past and present sometimes co-exist even in the same paragraph, and they co-exist not just as elements of grammar but in a psychological sense too: "Por la mañana he andado hoy a la ventura ... En algunos sitios me sorprende un olor a campo ... que me transporta con la imaginación a nuestra finca de Moscú" (p. 112). What Sacha does becomes a simple pretext for what she writes. Her external reality becomes an internal reality as she transforms her life into words.

In the preceding paragraphs I have identified five techniques used by Baroja in Part II of the novel to characterize Sacha's narration. These techniques comprise: (i) delicately stylized descriptions of natural objects; (ii) evocation of mood by the choice of particular adjectives or nouns; (iii) philosophical and personal reflections; (iv) references to other people which indirectly betray the state of mind of the writer; (v) rendering past actions in the present tense. All five techniques are employed again in Part III of the novel, in Sacha's diary.

Stylized descriptions of nature are much less frequent, since Sacha spends more time indoors, but a few examples can still be found: "álamos ... que parecen llamas cobrizas que salen de la tierra" (p. 131); "la ría brillaba bajo el cielo lleno de nubes plateadas" (p. 176).

The evocation of mood is if anything more pronounced. The

word *tristeza* and its derivatives *triste, entristecer* and *tristemente* make some fifteen appearances in Sacha's diary and are used to describe people's appearances, thoughts and utterances, buildings, landscapes, Christmas eve, and even the national deficiencies of the Spaniards. The blind minstrel and his family are described as having "un aire trágico"; the sun shines "de una manera mágica"; the night air has "una suavidad de caricia"; the plains of eastern Germany are enveloped in "una niebla melancólica". Melancholy, too, is the impression which an old song makes on Sacha, while the strong light and the warm air of an Andalusian afternoon produce in her "una impresión de languidez y de nostalgia" (p. 147).

Philosophical and personal reflections gain in both frequency and intimacy in the diary. Some of the reflections are sparked off by the symbol on the shield which so impresses Sacha and which she often recalls, and some by the lack of warmth she finds in her marriage. Her fleeting moments of hope and expectation are described with delicate imagery:

> Como la alondra que levanta el vuelo al amanecer, mi corazón se ha sentido con alas y ha volado lleno de esperanza al entrar en Andalucía. (p. 139)

> ... me sentía también ahora como crisálida que va a romper su envoltura para lanzarse al espacio ... (p. 141)

Her melancholy moods are described in terms more stark and forceful:

> Una serie de pensamientos tristes me angustian y sobrecogen ... Tengo el corazón oprimido. (p. 146)

> Me parece que estoy convaleciente de alguna enfermedad ... (p. 147)

In her references to other people in Part III, Sacha continues indirectly to betray her own state of mind quite clearly. When she describes the grain merchant with whom she has to share a train compartment as being utterly indifferent to other people's welfare, she cannot help establishing a comparison with her own husband, whose lack of consideration is soon to emerge fully in her diary. While in Italy she had criticized the sentimentality of the Italians as shallow and artificial, a criticism which reflected her own antipathy towards Amati; now she criticizes the lack of *efusión* in

Spaniards, which reflects her own disappointment in Velasco, who fails to provide the human warmth for which she craves. The case of Arcelu provides a good illustration of this technique, for Sacha, finding in him a means of communication, ascribes to him characteristics which are typical of herself: *tristeza, desconcierto, desilusión, dolor, enfermedad del análisis*. Shortly after entering her life, Arcelu comes to dominate her diary. She finds in him a kindred spirit who gives her the attention her husband denies her. He represents a possibility of finding what has been missing in her life all along: a spiritual association. That is why she gives their conversations so much space in her diary. He fills a gap in her life, and therefore in her writing.

Finally, the habit of rendering past actions in the present tense persists in Part III. One example will suffice. In chapter VI she relates her first evening in Seville, beginning with the past tense, "fuimos a dar una vuelta", and ending in a similar fashion, "volvimos todavía temprano". But in between, her impressions are conveyed mostly in the present tense, so that "dimos varias vueltas . . . y luego nos sentamos en un café" is followed by "desde la ventana del café *veo* . . ." (p. 140). As she sits in her hotel room later that night she re-creates the past in her mind: "Hemos salido del café. Son cerca ya de las diez de la noche y muchas tiendas están abiertas. Sigue el eterno ir y venir de la gente. Un relojero trabaja todavía delante del cristal del escaparate . . ." (pp. 140–1). By contemporizing her experiences Sacha betrays the way in which she tries to give an artistic or literary value to her aimless existence.

All these various techniques used by Baroja in Sacha's letters and diaries strongly suggest that Sacha's writings should be taken not as a record of events but as an artistic transformation of reality with the attendant revelation of a particular personality. Everything that Sacha writes is so much evidence against her; what she puts down is her whole personality: her illusions and disillusions, her anxieties and her loneliness, her sensibilities and emotional weaknesses, the failure of her personal relationships, the emptiness of her life, and the refuge and consolation of art. Even Arcelu's quaint theories and opinions, which do not appear to characterize Sacha in any way, are there because Arcelu acquires a special significance in her life. Sacha fills her writings totally, her spiritual presence dominates everything. It is her voice and hers alone that is heard.

There are thus two distinct narrative voices in *El mundo es ansí*. One is heard in Part I and can be related to the figure of the editor-narrator of the prologue, who can in turn be regarded as an authorial persona. In Parts II and III we still have the same author, Baroja, but the voice is rather different: this time Baroja has made a real effort to eliminate the personality of the editor-narrator. And this he does by introducing in Parts II and III several distinguishing narrative characteristics. No precise equivalent of the techniques which I have identified above is to be found in Part I, where the narrator is a different person. There, the reflections are rather different in tone: iconoclastic, mocking and superior; the references to other people are blunt and at times even openly disdainful; there is no sustained or contrived evocation of mood by the choice of particular words, nor is the present tense ever used to describe past events. The closest we come to Sacha's technique is in the description of the landscape (see pp. 74, 77, 87, 93); but the narrator's descriptions either lack the delicacy of Sacha's or are immediately preceded by a reference to Sacha as an observer (as is the case in the first three of the four passages referred to), so that we see the landscape in terms of the effect it has on Sacha herself.

It is time to summarize the narrative technique employed by Baroja in *El mundo es ansí* as I have outlined it in this and the preceding chapter. It is a technique in which the use of significant detail is of paramount importance and which turns out to be more complex than might appear at first sight. It is, moreover, a technique which poses important and intriguing questions about Baroja's artistic preoccupations, questions which I shall attempt to answer in the final chapter.

The narrative technique in this novel is tied up in the first place with the character of the protagonist herself. Sacha Savarof regards life – or at any rate her own – much as she regards art: as something to be analysed and understood. But her intellectual awareness is countered by her emotional confusion, and the consequent problems lead her to the attempted objectification of those problems through an artistic medium: the written word. Self-expression becomes creation, life becomes art. Sacha's need to express herself becomes part of her characterization; it *is* ultimately her characterization. But Sacha is not an exhibitionist; nor is she a mystifier. She may share with her creator the compulsion to translate life into words, but she cannot share the ulterior motive: publication. Baroja needed the former without the latter; he needed to allow the character to create itself, but not to create an image of itself, as a professional writer aware of his readers almost inevitably does. What Sacha Savarof writes is not destined for publication. The very nature of her activity calls for an editor, hence the role of the editor-narrator in the story. But Baroja does not content himself with using the editor for the traditional reason of structural verisimilitude, since the pretence of an autonomous narration is not sustained. He does not create a purely fictional editor-narrator, but one invested with Baroja's own authorial traits and powers. We thus have an editor who has not abandoned his authorial position, and conversely an author who functions also as an editor. This authorial representative has his own point of view in the novel, a point of view which is characterized by irony. Though seemingly existing on the same plane as the fictional characters, the editor-narrator betrays a clear feeling of superiority in his attitude towards them. This creates an impression of detachment, a distancing effect which is naturally attributable to the author himself. Baroja apparently wishes to imply a distinction between himself and his creatures, and this he does by novelizing the perspective from which he himself as author regards his fiction. He appears to want us to understand that we are observing a creation which is not the same looked at from the inside (i.e. from the vantage point of the characters) as looked at from the outside (i.e. from the vantage point of the author).

The ironic detachment of the narrator, and concomitantly his authorial omniscience, tend to be lost as we move closer to the central character. When Sacha takes over the narration, irony and detachment give way to tender melancholy and concern about herself and life in general. The character achieves a degree of independence and autonomy, but the control and point of view of the editor-narrator are intermittently established in his personal interventions (final chapter of Part II and epilogue). But if the narrator remains ultimately in control of the narration, in the end he too seems to succumb to the fiction and is affected by the story which Sacha tells of herself. That the narrator is moved by Sacha's self-revelation is evidenced not merely by the simple fact that he edits her writings (that after all is a prerequisite) and by his own admission in the prologue of the impression that Sacha's letter had on him, but also by his own evocation of Sacha's refrain in the closing words of the book. The shifting narrative distance throughout the book is thus in the end stabilized when the narrator's ironic detachment from the characters gives way to a feeling of pity and understanding as he and the reader watch appalled while Sacha shuts herself off from life ("se encerró en su cuarto") and gives herself up to her private world of grief and symbol. The book ends at the point where communication ceases, and the final impression on the reader is one of emptiness and desolation.

6 *Life, art and truth: the relationship creator-creation in* El mundo es ansí

In the previous chapter I put forward the view that there are two separate and distinct narrative voices in *El mundo es ansí* : one, mocking, smug, self-confident, belonging to the editor-narrator; the other, sentimental, melancholy, uncertain, belonging to the fictional protagonist. But what, if any, is the relationship between these two voices? And why has Baroja thought it necessary to distinguish one from the other? And why has he deliberately associated one of them with himself?

These questions do not have easy answers. We are dealing here with problems of interpretation which are by their very nature intractable. Few modern writers are willing to tell their readers or their critics what the particular meaning of a work is, in all likelihood because they are not very clear themselves. On the whole it is easy to infer the authorial norm in nineteenth-century fiction, and this constitutes a helpful guide to the reader. In twentieth-century fiction the authorial norm is much harder to pin down: authors prefer to leave the reader to his own devices while they themselves either abstain from commitment, or commit themselves in such a variety of ways that the reader is left in a quandary. This has given rise to a great amount of interpretative disparity and critical debate, and in the case of major works, like those of James Joyce for instance, key issues affecting their interpretation remain to this day unresolved and the subject of controversy. At first sight Baroja's blunt disposition and forthright views on many subjects might seem to discount the possibility of any such evasiveness on his part, but the truth is that once Baroja stops writing about other people and their work and writes instead about himself and his own art his customary outspokenness evaporates. What is surprising about Baroja's many writings on the novel is how few direct and concrete references they contain to his work. He either evades fundamental issues, or, when he does raise such issues, provides us with exasperatingly cryptic statements. It is usually when he is writing on other subjects and his defences are down that he indirectly provides us with some valuable clues. This coyness of Baroja's when writing about his art must naturally be in some way connected with the novels themselves, or with his uncertainties about them, and indeed many of them have features that appear odd and at times perhaps even arbitrary, but also curiously suggestive, features that seem to want to tell us something and that demand explanations. The critic has to seek possible explanations by considering both the effects produced by the techniques or devices employed in the particular work in question and the preoccupations of the novelist in other works chronologically close to it.

El mundo es ansí is without a doubt the most esoteric of the novels of Baroja's first period, full of ambiguities and half-hints, but I believe we can go a long way towards deciphering its meaning if we consider it as a novel of crisis, a personal document on the part of the artist, or more precisely as the culmination of a process of artistic preoccupation that had been bothering Baroja to the point of obsession: the relationship creator-creation in a work of art. As I explained in chapter II, several of the novels that precede *El mundo es ansí* are in some way connected with this question; this is certainly true of *César o nada*, of *Las inquietudes de Shanti Andía* and of *El árbol de la ciencia*. What all these novels have in common with one another and with *El mundo es ansí* is that they reflect the increasing use their author is making of auto-biographical material. Could these experiences, transposed from the world of the author to the world of the fictional characters, have any objective value in themselves or be given such a value?

Influenced perhaps by the prevailing symbolist view of art, several writers of the late nineteenth and early twentieth centuries (among them Guy de Maupassant, Henry James, George Santayana and, much more to the point here, José Ortega y Gasset with whom Baroja carried on a friendly polemic and who is the only one of his contemporaries of whom Baroja grudgingly admitted to have stood in intellectual awe) had been saying that an artistic creation should never be the direct real-life experience of the artist himself, but should be so formulated as to create a distance between creator and creation. The problem is, as Baroja himself realized, that the artist's contemplative gaze is turned inwards. When I think about the world, what I see is, in Baroja's words, "el modo de representarse en mi inteligencia las cosas del mundo" (*OC*, V, p. 11). The writer exists first as a person, and his writing is inevitably an extension of his person. Should he therefore disguise the fact, or openly, or tacitly, admit it? And if art is necessarily an extension of the writer's self, can that art be given an objective validity?

The dilemma, with its ensuing artistic crisis, may well have stemmed in the particular case of Baroja from the irreconcilability of Kantian philosophy and the social value of art. Baroja refused to accept that art had an end in itself, and claimed that it was worthy only in so far as it dealt with general human values, with matters of universal human concern (this he had in common with Galdós). But at the same time (and unlike Galdós), he had been very profoundly influenced by the Kantian view that ultimately the individual consciousness is all the reality there is, that the brain acts as a separating membrane between the individual and the world, and that there is no guarantee that what we perceive is an objective reality with equal validity for all of us. Baroja's aspiration to be a writer who dealt in matters of importance to humanity was undermined by his belief that his world was his own and nobody else's.

There was one possible way out of the dilemma: Schopenhauer's view of art. Schopenhauer claimed that art was a valid form of knowledge, not of the material world but of the 'Ideas' underlying it. If the artist could somehow apprehend that particular reality – that is to say, the reality of the world considered as 'Idea' – then he could communicate that knowledge. But how could this be achieved? This is Schopenhauer's answer:

> . . . it is certain that, if it is possible for us to raise ourselves from knowledge of particular things to that of the Ideas, this can happen only by a change taking place in the subject. Such a change is analogous and corresponds to that great change of the whole nature of the object, and by virtue of it the subject, in so far as it knows an Idea, is no longer individual.[27]

By this Schopenhauer really means (as he then goes on to explain in his usual roundabout and undisciplined way) that the artist must become pure perception, must cut his emotive links with the world

[27] Schopenhauer, *The World as Will and Representation*, translated by E. F. J. Payne, 2nd edition (New York, 1969), Vol. I, p. 176.

he is representing, must stand back and contemplate. We can see at once where this leads: to ironic detachment.[28]

The wilful manipulation of authorial distance is one of Baroja's most characteristic devices, at any rate during the period 1910–1912. In *César o nada* an authorial figure comes into the prologue in the guise of "el médico de Cestona" to argue with the protagonist, while in *El árbol de la ciencia* Baroja is becoming so closely identified with the protagonist (or fears that he is) that halfway through he dons his doctor Iturrioz outfit and all but flattens Hurtado's philosophy of life. In *El mundo es ansí* the technique persists and intensifies. It persists because Baroja has created, within the work, the figure of the editor-narrator with whom he invites us to associate him; and it intensifies because this authorial persona exhibits an attitude of ironic detachment towards the other characters.

The writer figure of the prologue begins by pretending that the story he has to tell is not of his making, but the way he proceeds to tell it draws attention to his presence. Baroja adopts the position of the ironist who undermines the truth of what he says even as he says it. There is some connection between the book that the Spanish writer sends to Sacha and Sacha's own preoccupations: "En su libro he creído ver reflejada la vida española que tanto me ha perturbado ..." (p. 41). Could it perhaps be significant that Sacha writes *he creído ver*? Is Baroja asking whether, or questioning his readers' belief that, his books do that? On the one hand there is the desire, even the need, to interpret the outside world, on the other the realization that there is no objective reality which a novel or any work of art can state. It is not "la vida española" but "la representación de la vida ambiente en mi conciencia" (*OC*, V, p. 229) that Baroja offers. And this time the vision of the outside world – that is to say the vision that we get through Sacha – will be clearly subsumed in the vision of a particular consciousness.

The device of the editor-narrator as used by Baroja in *El mundo es ansí* has therefore two effects. Firstly, it provides a consciousness through which those parts of the story not told by Sacha herself can

---

[28] Another great modern ironist much influenced by Schopenhauer's view of art is the German novelist Thomas Mann. For Mann's equation of objectivity in the Schopenhauerian sense with irony, see his essay "The Art of the Novel", in *The Creative Vision*, edited by Block and Salinger (New York, 1960).

be filtered. Far from the story appearing to 'tell itself' it appears very much to 'be told', to be the work of a very particular story-teller. Secondly, it invites us to identify the author with the voice of the editor-narrator; and having identified him with that voice we are less likely to identify him with the other voice, that of the protagonist. Both of these aspects are of fundamental importance. I shall discuss each in turn, taking the second point first, and then attempt to explain where the connection lies.

The distancing effect achieved by Baroja in his work has been most usefully commented upon by Biruté Ciplijauskaité although without any very specific examples being adduced. After outlining some of the ways in which Baroja creates a distance between himself and his work, Ciplijauskaité concludes:

> La actitud irónica, una actitud que crea distancia, es frecuente-mente característica de hombres tímidos: les sirve como auto-defensa. Ya se ha comentado que en el fondo Baroja tenía una tendencia hacia lo sentimental, hacia lo íntimo, como lo demue-stran sus primeras obras y su admiración por Bécquer y Ver-laine. En sus años maduros, hace mención de esta 'enfermedad' y trata de comprender el cambio gradual ocurrido: "¿Cómo y cuándo mi sensiblería y mi sentimentalismo se convirtieron en burla y en tendencia irónica? No lo sé a punto fijo." La actitud irónica en Baroja se puede considerar, pues, como una máscara que nunca se convirtió en figura verdadera (recordemos que elogia el humorismo sentimental), pero que le ayudó a forjarse un estilo muy personal e inconfundible. (*4*, pp. 268–9)

Ironic distance, then, can be regarded as a smokescreen erected by an author who knows or believes that his writing is but an endless self-acting, a perpetual self-exposure, and who feels that some element of dissimulation is necessary. In *El mundo es ansí* the manipulation of authorial distance has this protective func-tion, but in this case the question is rendered more complex as a result of Baroja's allowing the protagonist to narrate her own experiences and to narrate them in a particular way. For in a curious and suggestive way, Sacha, as a writer seeking to estab-lish the truth about herself and her environment, seems to mirror Baroja's position as a writer. Having read what Sacha writes about playing a role, about the spectator who is also the actor, about the phenomenon of playing up to one's public image, about the need for restraint in the expression of feelings, it is impossible to avoid the suspicion that Baroja is referring cryptically to his own role as a writer.

Sacha begins her diary by comparing her own situation with that of Vera Petrovna. Both women have got married at about the same time, Vera having married the man earlier rejected by Sacha. Sacha has married an artist, whereas Vera has married a scientist. As a result of their respective marriages, Vera "está en terreno más firme que yo . . .; yo, en cambio, no veo claro en mi porvenir" (p. 128). In the novel immediately preceding *El mundo es ansí*, *El árbol de la ciencia*, a work with a strongly autobiographical flavour, Baroja had told the story of a man passionately committed to science whose faith in the subject had been shattered and who as a result had committed suicide. Science had provided him with a philosophy of life, with an intelligible and objective view of existence, but in the end his vision was defeated and this had left him in an ideological void. The strange words with which the novel closes, "había en él algo de precursor", can be seen to acquire meaning if transposed from the fictional world of Hurtado to the real world of Baroja. Hurtado's suicide at the end of the book may be interpreted symbolically as Baroja's own failure to find in the scientific view of existence a satisfactory way of life. The rejection of the scientific approach to life and the concomitant loss of security that adherence to a solid system of beliefs and convictions brings – the security which Vera finds in her "hombre de ciencia" but which Sacha rejects – is followed in *El mundo es ansí* by the adoption of an artistic approach to life. Andrés Hurtado represents the scientific side of Baroja's life and personality with all its attendant problems; Sacha Savarof represents the artistic side of Baroja with all its doubts and anxieties. Hurtado is a precursor because his death points to the onset of the 'other' Baroja. I do not want to imply that one can divide Baroja chronologically into two phases, an earlier scientific one and a later artistic one, since these two aspects of his interests and personality quite clearly co-exist from the very beginning. What I do say is that *El árbol de la ciencia* dramatizes the notion of the scientific approach to life and *El mundo es ansí* that of the artistic approach. Both books, taken together, represent faithfully the dual nature of Baroja's writings: observation of an outward reality and representation of an inner imagination, objectivity and subjectivity in a never-ending dialectical interplay. Thus, in *El mundo es ansí*, beneath the deliberate dissociation between author and fictional protagonist there lurks an involvement at a deeper level, a latent allusion to the artistic representation of the creative self.

Sacha Savarof translates life into art: the observation of the outside world serves as the basis for an exclusively artistic and highly personal construction. Sacha herself brings up the question of the relationship between art and life in her letters to Vera (Part II, chapter IV), but her apparent devaluation of art becomes totally suspect when her writings are examined closely, and could even be regarded as another of Sacha's self-delusions. On receiving Sacha's letters, Vera twice tells her friend that she is being carried away by her artistic bent, and I would argue that it is Vera, with her practical approach ("con su buen sentido" in the editor-narrator's words), who senses the truth about Sacha. In her letters to Vera, Sacha is indulging in artistic fabrication, and the whole correspondence, properly read, amounts to a huge pretence on the part of Sacha (though not necessarily a conscious one). "Aunque quisiera hablarte de mis sentimientos, no podría ... Todas mis impresiones actuales están sólo en las pupilas, no han pasado más adentro" (p. 105). This is clearly not so: Sacha's descriptions exude feeling, and the impression of a perceiving mind is very strong; in addition we find Sacha's philosophizing interspersed throughout the descriptions. Both the letters and the diary are artistic creations, with their delicate descriptions, their melancholy philosophizing, their stylized redaction, their contrived exquisiteness in many instances. Furthermore, the way Sacha confuses art and life is noticeable in many of the things she says. "Los libros son un poco de opio en nuestra vida sin vida. El viejo Tolstoi, cuando habla con desprecio del arte y de las complicaciones de la vida moderna, creo que tiene bastante razón" (p. 107). But Tolstoy happens to be one of the great artists of the art of writing, as Sacha herself implicitly acknowledges later when she takes María Karolyi to task for believing that Tolstoy "es poco artista" (p. 114). A similar confusion between art and life arises when she compares Dostoyevski and D'Annunzio: "Un d'Annunzio, repleto de cultura clásica, sería superior en espíritu a un Dostoievski, que vivió muchos años en presidio, y no creo que a nadie que conozca a los dos se le ocurra compararlos" (p. 114). Of course not, but the indubitable superiority of one over the other does not depend on the fact that one happened to go to prison while the other was immersing himself in classical culture. And just in case anyone would wish to make the perfectly reasonable objection that this confusion is not intended but arises purely because of Baroja's faulty reasoning, let me adduce one final example where no such possibility exists. Sacha affirms the superiority of Murillo over El Greco on the grounds that Murillo's figures are realistic, they are true to life, whereas El Greco's figures are extravagantly out of shape, not true to life. Baroja himself most certainly did not believe this, as D. L. Shaw reminds us in a note to the text (p. 187). The point of the incident is that it highlights yet again the confusion in Sacha between art and life. Indeed there are other instances of this hesitation and confusion in Sacha, and they point to a deep preoccupation on the part of the novelist with this fundamental and intricate question of the relationship between art and life. There is therefore a profound connection between author and fictional protagonist in *El mundo es ansí*. It is not, of course, that the character is the author, as Baroja misleadingly seemed to suggest when he once declared that his main characters were based on himself, and as some commentators have blandly repeated; it is that the character is an allegorical dramatization of the problems of the author. The connection lies, not in the biography or in the personal traits of the fictitious character, but in her activity. Sacha Savarof is Baroja's novelistic exploration and representation of his own problem of preserving reality while creating art. The reality offered to us by Sacha is that created by her own imagination; she purports to write about Florence and about Spain when what she is really doing is projecting herself, revealing her personality. And as for Sacha, so for Baroja.

The editor-narrator, I earlier said, provides a consciousness through which the story of Sacha Savarof is passed on. This is the essence of his role. He functions as a centre of consciousness and not as a conventional device for the attainment of structural verisimilitude. We can now see why Baroja has deliberately abstained from filling in those obvious gaps in Sacha's story and from providing all those missing explanations of how the editor obtained the necessary information (discussed in chapter IV). It is not so much that Baroja cannot be bothered to spell it all out, but that it would be irrelevant and even misleading to do so. What we get in *El mundo es ansí* is the story of Sacha handed down through an experiencing consciousness. What is important is the narrator's experience of Sacha; therefore what we get is what is relevant to that experience; everything else is sacrificed. Only a minimum of information is offered, just enough to establish a connection between protagonist and narrator (the starkness of chapter III of the prologue is quite striking). We can assume if we like that the narrator had access to other sources of information; that he visited Madame Frossard several times; that he also visited Vera Petrovna in Geneva; that in this city he also made the acquaintance of Klein (all of which is what any interested person would have done in real life). All these and more explanations could have been provided by Baroja with the greatest of ease. But they would have been irrelevant to his purpose and a mere distraction. Baroja's way of infusing realism into a literary invention is not to think up spurious reasons and fictitious explanations, but to make it come alive in an experiencing consciousness. And with characteristic honesty he even identifies that consciousness with the only one he knows: his own.

Sacha's writings – her vision of the world – are no more than a projection of her own individuality. But they have a reader in the form of the editor-narrator who plays a crucial role in bringing her story to light. This narrator, endowed with his own mentality or outlook, maintains his distance: his consciousness remains separate from Sacha's, and as editor he has the last word. He is interested not in the truth of Sacha's vision of the world, which does not coincide with his own, but only in the truth of Sacha herself. Thus, while Sacha's world is her own, she in turn becomes the narrator's world. He works his way towards Sacha as in fulfilment of his role as editor he reads and re-creates her writings, so that in the end his consciousness is almost congruent with hers. The narrator does not admit the validity of Sacha's vision; he admits the validity of its expression. Sacha's subjective vision is given an objective validity by virtue of being accepted by a different consciousness.

When Alain Robbe-Grillet, the contemporary French novelist and theoretician of the genre, said that the artist is a man with nothing to say what he meant was that it is the artist in the man who speaks and not the man himself. As a man, the writer may lead a dull existence, no more and perhaps a great deal less interesting than those of other men. In his creative role as a writer he has to make his own reality. The truth is not in what he writes about, but in having written it; the truth is the truth of art, not of reality. The writer's experience as a person is nothing except as it is led by his creative consciousness; and having been led by this creative consciousness it is transported to another sphere of existence. Art and life are separate categories, each true in its own ways, but they are lies when judged by each other's criteria. Baroja, whose commitment to truth in all spheres of existence was obsessive, had to face a dilemma: how to account for the relationship between the truth of art and the truth of everyday existence, between the world he inhabited as an ordinary man in an unconscious universe and the worlds he created consciously as a writer. Baroja's novels veer violently from subjective 'poetry' to social document, and this reflects the struggle going on within an artist who wants to imbue his writings with some sort of truth that will have universal validity.

In *El mundo es ansí* Baroja has dramatized the process of artistic creation. As she consigns her experiences to paper, Sacha converts her life into art. Her imagination transforms reality, and that reality, whatever it may have been, is not accessible. The truth of Sacha's writings is not to be found in an anterior reality. By the time the writing passes on to the editor-narrator there is no anterior reality, because Sacha's representation of the world is not a neutral one. Art is not neutral, any more than the human mind itself; indeed, even words, the building bricks of the literary arts, are not neutral. And yet language is the only source of the dialectical relationship between the self and the world. The reality for the editor-narrator is not Sacha's vision but Sacha's writings. He may look ironically upon a world which he knows to be a world of words, but he accepts the reality of its effects. The editor-narrator's role is thus a creative one: he confers a particular reality on Sacha's writings. The move from Sacha to the narrator represents the move from unconscious creation to creative consciousness, where the creator is aware of his role as a maker of artifacts.

It is now a simple matter to transpose this world back to its maker. Sacha's experience represents the raw material of all art: the world in which everything exists, the world in its inchoate, uninterpreted and uninterpretable form, a world which will not yield up its secret and which cannot be corresponded to. Sacha's writings represent the subjective interpretation of the world, that is to say the artist's attempt to reduce the irreducible by capturing his highly personal reaction to the world of his own existence. The narrator's reading of Sacha's writings represents the more objective examination of this highly subjective vision, as the artist begins to undergo the *desdoblamiento*, the unfolding of himself into the teller and the reader, of which Baroja speaks. The narrator's irony represents a detachment from that subjective vision, a realization that that initial vision has no objective validity. But this stepping back – the completion of the Schopenhauerian inversion of subject and object – enables the artist to consider that vision as a world in itself. The narrator's publication of Sacha's account represents the acceptance of the validity of art, a validity which is independent of the truth of the world, whatever that truth may have been.

In so far as one can hold beliefs in such a vaporous and ever-changing sphere as that of literary interpretation, I would end by asserting mine to the effect that *El mundo es ansí* has little to do with *noventaiochista* ideology and a great deal to do with art. I see it as the creation of a writer who is tormented by the question of truth in his art and who reflects his situation in the story he tells and in the way he tells it. The book is an exploration of the relationship between art and life, between an individual consciousness and the objective world, between an author and his work. It is only when seen as such that it acquires real meaning, and even perhaps poignancy, the poignancy not of a fictitious character but of a man to whom writing was his life and who had come to suspect that his art was based on an illusion, another of those *mentiras vitales* which he, too, like his characters, was forced to defend "con entusiasmo" because he had nothing else left. By the time he concluded *El mundo es ansí*, Baroja was already seeking refuge from his torment in historical research. So perhaps in the end he followed his own advice: "¿Para qué rascar en la purpurina? ¿Para qué analizar el oropel?" (p. 87).

Bibliographical note

1. Andrenio: "El mundo es ansí", in *Baroja y su mundo*, edited by Fernando Baeza (Madrid, 1961), Vol. II, pp. 52–4. A newspaper review, laudatory but superficial.

2. Azorín: *"El mundo es ansí"*, in *Pío Baroja. El escritor y la crítica*, edited by Javier Martínez Palacio (Madrid, 1974), pp. 409–12. A newspaper review that has the merit of pointing out the clash between the aesthetic and the spontaneous reactions to life in Baroja.

3. Cardona, Rodolfo: "En torno a *El mundo es ansí*", *Cuadernos Hispanoamericanos*, nos 265–7 (1972), 562–74. A disconcerting essay which combines interesting insights with serious misreadings in a loose framework of commentary.

4. Ciplijauskaité, Biruté: *Baroja, un estilo* (Madrid, 1972). Does not deal directly with *El mundo es ansí*, but almost certainly the best book on the art and style of Baroja. The final chapter is of fundamental importance.

5. Flores Arroyuelo, Francisco J.: *Las primeras novelas de Pío Baroja* (Murcia, 1967), pp. 115–19. Mostly descriptive, but makes the very relevant point that Sacha's language is meant to reflect her state of mind.

6. García de Nora, Eugenio: *La novela española contemporánea*, 2nd edition (Madrid, 1963), Vol. I, pp. 176–7. Of very limited value, but does suggest that *El mundo es ansí* reveals the 'inner' Baroja.

7. González López, Emilio: *El arte narrativo de Pío Baroja: las trilogías* (New York, 1971), pp. 226–36. Derivative and superficial.

8. Patt, Beatrice: *Pío Baroja*, TWAS, Spain, 146 (New York, 1971), pp. 122–5. A superficial analysis in a very conventional book.

9. Probyn, Hugh: "Pío Baroja: Aspects of the Development of his Work 1900–1912", Unpublished M.Phil dissertation, University of Leeds, 1976. A most useful study of some Barojan techniques with an excellent chapter on the use of irony.

10. Rodgers, Eamonn: "Realidad y realismo en Baroja: el tema de la soledad en *El mundo es ansí*", *Cuadernos Hispanoamericanos*, nos 265–7 (1972), 575–590. Sensitive, perceptive, almost certainly the best study of this particular novel.

11. Shaw, D. L.: Critical introduction to the edition of *El Mundo es ansí* published by Pergamon Press (Oxford, 1970). Adopts an ideological approach. Essential as an alternative interpretation to the one put forward in this Critical Guide.

12. Sordo, Enrique: "Dos novelas singulares: *César o nada* y *El mundo es ansí*", in *Baroja y su mundo*, edited by Fernando Baeza (Madrid, 1961), Vol. I, pp. 148–56. A short, useful essay. Argues that the author has tried to eliminate his presence by adopting objectivist techniques.